NEW PLAYS FROM THE CARIBBEAN
(FRANCOPHONE EDITION)

NEW PLAYS FROM THE CARIBBEAN (FRANCOPHONE EDITION)

Edited by

Stéphanie Bérard

with

Frank Hentschker

Martin E. Segal Theatre Center Publications

Frank Hentschker, Executive Director

Martin E. Segal Theatre Center Publications
New York, © 2022

All rights reserved. Except for brief passages quoted in newspaper, magazine, radio or television reviews, no part of this book may be reproduced in any form or by any means, electronic or mechanical, including photocopying or recording, or by an information storage and retrieval syst, without permission in writing from the publisher.

Professionals and amateurs are hereby warned that this material, being fully protected under the Copyright Laws of the United States of America and all other countries of the Berne and Universal Copyright Conventions, is subject to a royalty. All rights including, but not limited to, professional, amateur, recording, motion picture, recitation, lecturing, public reading, radio and television broadcasting, and the rights of translation into foreign languages are expressly reserved. Inquiries concerning production rights should be addressed in advance, before rehearsals begin, to the Martin E. Segal Theatre Center, 365 5th Avenue, 3rd Floor, New York, NY 10016. Email: mestc@gc.cuny.edu.

Library of Congress Cataloging-in-Publication Data

Names: Bérard, Stéphanie, editor. | Hentschker, Frank, editor. | Gann, Amanda, translator.
Title: New plays from the Caribbean : (francophone edition) / edited by Stéphanie Bérard with Frank Hentschker ; [translators: Amanda Gann and six others].
Description: New York : Martin E. Segal Theatre Center Publications, [2022]
Identifiers: LCCN 2022007508 | ISBN 9781953892065 (paperback)
Subjects: LCSH: Caribbean drama (French)--21st century--Translations into English. | Caribbean drama (French Creole)--21st century--Translations into English. | LCGFT: Drama.
Classification: LCC PQ3947.5.E5 N49 2022 | DDC 842/.920809729--dc23/eng/20220411
LC record available at https://lccn.loc.gov/2022007508

Christopher Silsby, Production Editor

Ronad Cyrille, Cover Image

Christopher Silsby, Cover Design

© 2022 Martin E. Segal Theatre Center

NEW PLAYS FROM THE CARIBBEAN (FRANCOPHONE EDITION)

Edited by

Stéphanie Bérard
with
Frank Hentschker

Adoration
Jean-René Lemoine
HAITI/FRANCE

And the Whole World Quakes: Chronicle of a Slaughter Foretold
Guy Régis Jr
HAITI

Family
Gaël Octavia
MARTINIQUE

Ladjablès-Wild Woman
Daniely Francisque
MARTINIQUE

Street Sad
Luc Saint-Éloy
GUADELOUPE

The Day My Father Killed Me
Charlotte Boimare & Magali Solignat
GUADELOUPE

CONTENTS

Foreword — ix
Stéphanie Bérard

Adoration — 1
by Jean-René Lemoine
translation by Amanda Gann

And the Whole World Quakes:
Chronicle of a Slaughter Foretold — 23
by Guy Régis Jr
translation by Judith Miller

Family — 69
by Gaël Octavia
translation by Katharine Woff & Lucie Tiberghien

Ladjablès-Wild Woman — 117
by Daniely Francisque
translation by Danielle Carlotti-Smith

Street Sad — 157
by Luc Saint-Éloy
translation by Josh Cohen

The Day My Father Killed Me — 183
by Charlotte Boimare & Magali Solignat
translation by Amelia Parenteau

About the Playwrights — 215

About the Translatiors — 216

About the Editor — 218

About the Cover Artist — 218

Caribbean Theatre Project
ACT (Actions Caribéennes Théâtrales) Program — 219

FOREWORD

This unique anthology *New Plays from the Caribbean* represents a most significant and lasting part of the 2019 Caribbean Theater Project ACT (Actions Caribéennes Théâtrales)—co-organized by the Martin E. Segal Theatre Center in New York City, the theater company Siyaj from Guadeloupe, and myself. The project was inspired by a conversation I had in 2017 with Frank Hentschker, the director of the Segal Center. I was asking how we could find a way to make Francophone Caribbean theatre accessible to audiences outside of the insular perimeter and the French-speaking zone.

Following a blueprint of previous Segal Center international reading festivals, we decided to stage—over two days—elaborate readings of six plays from well-known and emergent Caribbean female and male theatre artists at the Martin E. Segal Theatre in December of 2019 in front of an American audience. I made twenty-two suggestions for plays to the New York distinguished Advisory Board composed of Alessandra Benedicty-Kokken, Nicole Birmann, Mária Brewer, Heather Denyer, Amin Erfari, Christian Flaugh, and Amaya Lainez Le Déan.

In the presence of the authors, the stage readings of the six plays from this extraordinary collection took place at the Martin E. Segal Theatre in December of 2019—seconds before the Time of COVID—in front of a live American audience. For the first time, the playwrights were able to hear their works in English. The Caribbean artists participated actively in artistic exchanges with New York directors and actors, engaging after each reading with always changing groups of distinguished guests: the brilliant festival dramaturge Candace Thompson-Zachery invited directors, curators, writers, academics, and New York theatre artists to join the discussion. ACT created a stunning, previously unseen dialogue with the American audience, opening a window onto how the plays are perceived and received outside of the Caribbean. It turned out that we became part of theatre history. To our knowledge, it was the very first time in the history of theatre that plays from three Caribbean islands were presented in a festival of their own.

By rejecting bygone East-West colonial relationship in favor of a new North-South axis, this collection of contemporary Caribbean plays highlights the historical and cultural links that tie the Americas together, that bind "ces terres sanguines consanguines" (bleeding lands, lands of inbreeding) to quote the Martinican poet Aimé Césaire in *Notebook of a*

Return to My Native Land. This New World, which shares the common legacy of colonialism and slavery, prefigures Édouard Glissant's concept of *Tout-Monde*—defined as a diverse totality that emerged from the unexpected and amazingly fruitful encounter of multiple cultures, races, languages, and "imaginaires." The famous writer and philosopher from Martinique taught at The Graduate Center CUNY where all the readings took place.

The anthology *New Plays from the Caribbean* exemplifies the Glissantian "Chaos Monde" and "mise en Relation." Engaged in a creative and innovative hybrid mixing of styles and languages (French, Creole, and some English), these playwrights present a politically engaged theatre while renewing dramatic forms, content, and aesthetics. These Caribbean dramatists tell us the stories and histories of contemporary Caribbean people by exploring passion, desire, and the collective experience of trauma and loss after a natural disaster. They denounce social, racial, and gender violence by staging real-life dramas and leading crime investigation.

New Plays from the Caribbean Plays is composed of six plays from Martinique, Guadeloupe, and Haiti written by playwrights each of whom has a personal and unique history with the Caribbean. Some were born or raised there and are now living in Europe (Gaël Octavia, Jean-René Lemoine, Luc Saint-Éloy) while others returned to their native islands after studying and working in Paris (Daniely Francisque, Guy Régis Jr); a few of them go back and forth between France and the Caribbean where they found a place of inspiration (Magali Solignat and Charlotte Boimare). The various and complex trajectories of these playwrights reflect the fluctuating and unpredictable movements of a contemporary kaleidoscopic reality and humanity in the contemporary Caribbean. Just as there is no assigned and fixed Caribbean identity, there is no single, unvarying Caribbean drama as such. There are multiple talents, multiple visions, and multiple aesthetics. Unveiling and revealing the rich and diverse production of contemporary Caribbean theatre, allowing new dramatic voices to be heard and to travel around the world, is the mission of this book.

Adoration (*L'Adoration*) by Jean-René Lemoine, explores the torments of passion. In a nightclub on a terrace overlooking the sea, a woman, Chine, and a man, Rodez, reflect on their relationship and their first encounter. Memories of desire, obsession, love, and hate mix with the sounds of far-away waves. Slowly, Chine unveils the inner legacy of a dangerous passion in which she lost herself. Jean-René Lemoine scrutinizes the infinitesimal movements of the soul; he plays a hypnotic musicality that soothes the reader/spectator who sinks into the throbbing back and forth of waves and memories.

And the Whole World Quakes: Chronicle of a Slaughter Foretold (*De toute la terre le grand effarement*) by Guy Régis Jr stages a cataclysmic world. Following on Beckett, two women characters, the Youngest and the Oldest, survivors of a catastrophe, stand on a hill overlooking a destroyed city. Both look upon the desolate landscape and hear the lamentations, prayers, and songs of the survivors. They count the shooting stars passing overhead and keep on talking to stay awake, to stay alive. Written after the 2010 earthquake in Haiti, the play questions how to continue living when all is destroyed.

Family (*Une vie familiale*) by Gaël Octavia explores and reveals the wounds and the fractures of an ordinary dysfunctional family. The father hides his homosexuality and tries to escape a stifling and suffocating family. The alcoholic, stay-at-home mother is jealous of the relationships her husband has with their children. Everyone struggles to play the games they are socially expected to play. The lies, secrets, and silences ultimately explode the constraining social conventions with which they have heretofore lived.

Ladjablès-Wild Woman by Daniely Francisque encounters a masked woman and an arrogant man who tries to seduce her during a night of Carnival in Martinique. Drunk with desire for the bewitching dancer, the heartless womanizer does not realize that the predator is slowly becoming the prey. Ingeniously interweaving Creole and French, song and dance, Daniely Francisque revisits the ritual of Carnival and turns the traditional figure of *ladjablès*, celebrated in popular beliefs, into a representative of the emancipated Martinican woman.

Street Sad (*Trottoir chagrin*) by Luc Saint-Éloy, places Marlène, a prostitute working the streets of Paris, downstage. She does not care about anything or anyone. One evening, she returns to the place where her brother Jeannot was murdered just a year before. There she meets a mysterious man with whom she starts a conversation. Marlène tells him her story and enters into a dangerous flirtation. Personal family memories cross into the collective history of oppression while the colonial past surges back to collide with present police violence.

The Day My Father Killed Me (*Le jour où mon père m'a tué*) co-authored by Charlotte Boimare and Magali Solignat is based on a true story of a singer who, a few years ago in Guadeloupe, murdered his own son. Devised as a documentary theatre work, the play's multiple voices narrate a diverse account of the crime. This co-written work takes a close look at the violence in one contemporary Caribbean society, creatively interweaving island gossip with social-media communication.

I want to acknowledge the engagement of the directors and actors as well as the invaluable contribution of the members of the Advisory Board who selected the plays. I warmly thank the talented translators who participated in this unpredictable and extraordinary journey.

I am deeply grateful to Elvia Gutiérrez, Administrative Director of Siyaj Company, Frank Hentscker, Executive Director of the Martin E. Segal Theatre Center, Nicole Birmann, from the Cultural Services of the French embassy, and Candace Thompson-Zachery for their highly precious collaboration.

Special thanks goes, also, to the Face Foundation, the Cultural Services of the French Embassy in New York, and the Contxto network in Paris for their support.

Stéphanie BÉRARD
ACT Curator

ADORATION
by
Jean-René Lemoine

HAITI/FRANCE

translation by Amanda Gann

Characters:

CHINA

RODEZ

Staging notes:

CHINA and RODEZ come from elsewhere. It does not matter which country. What matters is that they were born elsewhere, they live in France, France is where their story took place. But tonight, it is elsewhere that they meet again, precisely in that land where they were born.

A December 24th. The terrace of a night club, "La Batelière," overlooking the sea. The sound of waves mixes with the rhythmic beat of the music coming from inside.

A woman and a man alone on the empty terrace. The man has a bandage on one hand.

CHINA: But that look, the look you gave me, that look, the look that you gave me, that look was full of desire.

Silence.

> Stop right there, don't move, nothing will happen to you, as long as you stay within the halo of my sight, nothing will happen to you. Do you feel the wind moving through the leaves, bringing some relief after the humid afternoon?

Silence.

> You say nothing, you don't speak. You are there, standing still. There are wrinkles on your face, well, wrinkles, they're barely even wrinkles because you still look like a child. There are shadows that bespeak a terrible fatigue, a great weariness, that tell a tale of dread, that say you haven't been touched enough, caressed enough during all those years of your life. In fact, I don't even know how old you are.

RODEZ: Is that really important?

CHINA: It's important for me to tell you. If I were to stop speaking, I, I might throw myself into that—void, over there, a few feet away from us, so devouring, so tempting. I'm sorry, I have to, well, I had, I had to speak to you, tear you away from all those people, we had to talk, we had to talk. . .

RODEZ: We have already talked so much, said so many things. . .

CHINA: We have to talk again, but differently, with patience. The words have to go from me to you and they have to reach you, and you must not refuse them, you must not be frightened of them. . .

RODEZ: Why do you think they would. . .?

CHINA: They do frighten you, but not only my words. The ones that I am saying, that I am barely whispering, because I am exhausted, because it is dreadfully, shockingly late. These words that, fortunately, are lifted by the breeze that carries them from me to you like—butterflies, but also your words, the ones that you don't dare to say, the ones that you. . .

Silence.

There is something infinitely feminine in you that shakes me to the. . .

RODEZ: I'd better go.

CHINA: Why did you come? Why. . .?

RODEZ: I don't know, I don't know why I'm here.

Music is heard from inside. They fall silent.

CHINA: But when you looked at me, the first time, just before we were introduced to one another, that long look between you and me, don't tell me that it wasn't charged with desire.

RODEZ: But why bother talking about it, why bring it up again, rehash it all?

CHINA: And the next day, at four thirty-five, when we met again, when you entered my life, asking me where my pain came from, the immense pain that you had perceived from the first instant that you saw me, that pain that I didn't want to discuss even though I had a—terrible—desire to surrender myself to you, the next day, when we spent the evening talking, you talking and me trying not to say what you wanted to hear, what you already knew, when we were sat together, next to each other, almost touching, what did you want, what did you desire, you had no desire perhaps?

Silence.

You don't answer, you lower your head, I can't bear for you to lower your head, I can't bear the violence of your silence anymore, speak, for heaven's sake, speak, scream, shout, slap, hit, but do something, do something that would put an end to it, don't leave me, please. . . in this uncertainty, in this deadly in-between, this doubt, this unbelievable wait for you to say a word that would condemn me or exonerate me as soon as I heard it. You want to make me believe that I dreamt it, that I'm dreaming, that all of it is, has been, was, that all of it was only a dream. You want to keep pushing the boundaries until my reason falters. Why hound me like that? Answer me. Answer me! Why this assassination? Why do you keep looking at me—murderer—as if I were the one plunging in the spears, one after another, as if I were the one galloping circles around you, rearing back, stopping brutally, to—stab—you again, to make you bleed out the thick garnet of your substance, when it is you who hunted, tracked, stalked, snared, imprisoned me in the seething chains of your eyes and the evil clasp of your fingers. . . I have to collect my. . ., I have to gather what's left of my. . ., so that I don't go to pieces in front of you, at least not before I've said it all, clarified it all. Because tonight we will have to say everything, in the heat and in the wind.

They remain still, silent, statues.

How many hours did you spend next to me? Do you remember how many hours you spent at my place, standing or sitting, talking, your inquisitor's body carving slow, swirling lines that made the room smaller and made you larger. You knew the turmoil, you knew the earthquake that went off inside me but you kept on. You asked me where my suffering came from. I didn't want, I refused to tell you, how could I have said it?, I had spent my whole life hiding it, trying to mask it, and you thought—bold!—that you could blow it up in an instant, the shiny carapace of my life. What did you say, what did you say that night? You kept on repeating the word 'suffering', and I kept repeating, inwardly, I kept saying to myself, let him stop, let him stop, god!, let him stop, or I'm going to scream. And then you came over to me, very close to me, as is your habit, you didn't touch me, didn't even brush against me, but I didn't know, I didn't know yet that—that this was your fiendish habit. So I spoke to you about desire. I told you that there had been, there had been desire between us from the first moment that we looked at each other, before that person who was supposed to introduce us ever introduced us. I told you that the look I gave you, or that you gave me—how to know who committed the first offense—that this look had been so long that we had been obliged to speak, to break the tension somewhat. And then, you said that that look, that night, on that terrace, hadn't been the first look, that there had been one before, the very first look, the real first look in the love crime. I'm sorry, I have to stop. That music, that music makes me want to—drown myself.

Silence.

You said, and I had to admit it, wondering to what inexpressible nightmare I had relegated it, you said that it was inside that we had looked at each other, but that this look had been swift as a slash, bright as lightning; and all of a sudden I remembered, and I told you that you were right, that it was only later that we, I mean, that this second look happened, the one that—in my terrible unconscious—I had christened as the first. I told you—because everything was becoming clear and transparent like the ocean gulfs of our countries—I told you that after, after this original look, I went out onto the terrace to join some friends that I had seen through the window. But suddenly I realized it was you, and only you, my desire was following. Unconscious, ghost-like, I went out onto the terrace, thinking I was joining my friends, in order to find you, you and only you, you and nothing but you. You were sitting, alone, next to these people that suddenly I identified as—friends, but who were really only accomplices, unmoving tombstones that would, unbeknownst to them, help me to cross the ford. It's appalling how right you were that evening, when you were telling me about the day before. And it all came back to my mind like a tide crashing in. And that is when I remembered talking to my friends as a sleepwalker talks to the trees when she loses her way in a garden, or to the birds when she's walking softly on a roof. I was talking to my friends and I gave you a drawn-out look, at once so pure and so indecent, that we were obliged to—speak and you said to me, or I said to you—I don't remember who launched the attack: "I believe that we've met before". Of course that wasn't true. We had never met before. But to persuade ourselves for a moment that we had already met—somewhere other than in our dreams—in a real past, allowed us to make the situation bearable, and to keep looking at one another, through the words, without my friends worrying to see us standing silent for so long in the thick air of that late afternoon. It was you, I think you were the one who said it. . .

RODEZ: What did I say?

CHINA: "I believe that we've met," I think it was you. . .

RODEZ: Perhaps.

CHINA: And then she arrived, that friend who was supposed to—introduce us to one another. She said, surprised: "So you've already met?" We smiled, we lied, we said yes, we told her that we had met before. I've forgotten the rest. It was a. . . how can I put it?. . . until you asked me for a—meeting, under the—false—pretense that maybe—but that may be was never going to be—we would work together. And we agreed to meet at my place the next day, and the next day you were at my place at four thirty-five, late by five minutes, which drew themselves out so that they seemed to me like five weeks and at nine thirty-five you were still there, after five hours of bliss, let's call it bliss, hours so short that they seemed to me like five seconds, asking me to tell you about my suffering, to tell you everything, it's true that one can call it bliss, at least it was the only time that you were gentle to me, after it was only murder, or almost, and you sat down—oh!—close to me, and you knew that I. . . and you acknowledged that our first two looks—now so perfectly elucidated—had been absolute looks of desire and you stayed there, motionless, while storms battered my insides and I looked around for something to hold onto as the walls started to crumble little by little, so that I wouldn't be swept away in the earthquake that I've already told you about.

Silence.

> Don't move. Do not move. Don't move. I'm telling you not to. . . No, don't move.

We can hear the sea.

> Of course, there was someone in your life. It's always the same. There is always someone in the life of the person who could have entered ours. But what did it matter to me then, you had already entered mine never to leave again. I wasn't expecting anything, I mean, I thought that I no longer expected anything. I was content to count the seconds, to photograph each instant, because if, like me, you have vast experience with emptiness and adversity and then suddenly you recognize the glowing warmth of a moment that will mark you forever, you steal every fragment of gesture, every syllable uttered, so that you can project them for a long time, for weeks, even years after, onto the screen of memory.

Silence.

> Tornado of words, hurricanes that they give names to in our countries, that one I name after you, I call it Rodez, like you, I. . . I, I'm at a loss for words, I'm so overcome by the vertigo of you, we have to—yes, that's it—tonight we must have everything out between us, and tonight I will not abandon you, and you will not abandon me either until we have said it all, until we have annihilated one another, in the passion and spit of words, for lack of anything else, because there is nothing else and, to hear your silence, there never was.

Silence.

> Confess, I'm begging you, confess that you are on the brink, that you can't take it anymore, that you're like me, lost, alone, a flimsy little boat out on the. . . (*Silence*) You're crying.

Silence.

Then you left, you went home where certainly someone was waiting for you, or did you perhaps go somewhere else, yes that's it, someone was waiting for you somewhere else, you were even quite late because you had lost track of time, unaware of the danger posed by your presence in my apartment and—for those five, too short hours—unable to decide to leave and. . . Yes, yes. . . So you left, not without scribbling down your phone number which I didn't have yet because, naturally, as always, I was the one who had given mine and my address as well, at the risk that you wouldn't come and I would die suffocated by waiting for you. (*Silence*) Then I told you that I wouldn't call you, that I would rather you call me. And you slid into my arms and I leaned against your shoulder for a swift embrace from which you already seemed to be escaping and you looked at me and I held your gaze until—you—lowered your eyes because we both already knew that—I—had gone far beyond the pale of this story in which all you had left to do was come and go in your exhausting, violating way. I can't tell you the emptiness of my apartment after you had left, the sudden desire to break the rule that I myself had set, to call you, wherever you might be in the hostile city, in the place where they were keeping you hostage, so that I could implore you to come back to me at once because of course, from the moment that you stepped through my doorway, I accepted the fact that I could not live without you. How can I tell you about the days that followed, me in despair by the telephone like the heroine in some melodrama, making smaller and smaller circles around the telephone, reaching out my hand, brushing over, dialing the first few numbers, thinking better of it, dialing again, waiting hours on end for you to call, jumping whenever it would ring, trembling, stumbling, hesitant, desperate, letting the first few rings go, finally picking up, speechless, all my strength gone, only to realize that it wasn't you, it was someone else, sitting down so as not to be overcome with nausea, trying to reassure the person on the other line, who was startled to hear this voice suddenly become so gloomy, stitching my words back together with great difficulty, interrupting the intruder, cutting short the conversation, until I clumsily hung up the receiver so that I could wait some more, wait, wait, wait—wait for you and nothing but you. How can I tell you about those nights when I would come home exhausted and pulsating, rush over to the beloved then detested answering machine and you hadn't called. Me, foolish Madame Butterfly strewn across the white bedspread, fully dressed, made-up, motionless, like a still breathing Ophelia, staring at the ceiling like the endless foam of the ocean in our countries, exiled from myself, wild with rage, nursing the insult of not being reached, not being desired, me, abandoned, forgotten, consigned to the attic of your memory, wiped from your galaxy, definitively erased, oh! if you knew, if you knew what I had to suffer.

Silence.

"On go the days and on the weeks."
You didn't call.

Silence.

And then naturally, ineluctably, I found an excuse. I was playing at the theater. Therefore I had to invite you. I had to invite you because I was playing at the theater. You would have held it against me if I had deprived you of my art. And of course I felt calmed, fulfilled, satisfied, dispossessed of you, from the moment that I had a reason to call you. I had mourned you and I even let twenty-four hours pass, before phoning you. Your voice was deep, smooth and calm, smooth and calm on the telephone. Your phrase is carved into my heart. You said, "I didn't know if I should seek you or avoid you." That is what you said. Isn't it true, that you said that? Did you say that?

RODEZ: Yes, perhaps.

CHINA: What does that mean, perhaps?

RODEZ: Yes, of course. . .

CHINA: Did you. . .

RODEZ: . . . I must have. . .

CHINA: . . .say it or didn't you? Answer me. (*Silence.*) I asked you to answer me.

RODEZ: Let's go inside.

CHINA: No. Go inside if you like. I'm staying. I cannot go inside.

RODEZ: China, I'm tired.

CHINA: I am tired too.

RODEZ: China, it's late.

CHINA: Dreadfully late.

RODEZ: So then let's go inside, please, let's go inside, I don't feel very well.

CHINA: I can't, Rodez, I can't go in, don't you understand that I can't go inside?

RODEZ: But you aren't going to stay there, forever, for all eternity?

Long silence.

CHINA . . .

Long silence.

   (*To himself*). . . if I should seek you or avoid you.

CHINA: If you knew what I had to suffer. (*Silence*) You came to see me at the theater. You congratulated me, you had that carnivorous smile, you were neither trembling, nor worried, nor exhausted, you said some coherent things. Then suddenly, during the conversation, a hand grabbed you and you turned around slightly and you abandoned me there while a hand that wasn't yours placed itself on my shoulder, a mouth kissed my cheek, someone said something to me, and I, champagne glass in hand, responded like an automaton to the fingers and mouths that had just abducted me and I tried to hear the words you were saying, they came to me in bits from far off, so far, I was trying to follow you with my eyes but you were pulling away from my shores, carried by—the tide so that it was impossible for me to. . .I couldn't understand why you weren't coming back to me of your own free will, with the strength and the power of your body. I realized that you had simply come to watch me and that now that you had seen me, you felt free to leave. And then for a second, you were so far away from me, at the other end of the lobby, our eyes met and you smiled at me. So I stopped drinking and. . .

The sound of the sea. Silence.

When I took you in my mouth. . .

Silence.

Confess, confess it, Rodez, I'm begging you, confess at least that it's all true, that I'm not lying, that I'm not mistaken, because the longer I hear you say nothing, I get the sense that nothing happened, my reason starts to falter the longer I listen to you not speaking. Speak to me, Rodez, tell me.

Silence.

RODEZ: Let's go in.

CHINA: No, I don't want to, I don't want to, I don't want to go inside!

RODEZ: All of that is useless and. . .

CHINA: All of that is. . .

RODEZ: . . . absurd.

CHINA: Useless and absurd to you. Useless and absurd to you, Rodez, you're the one standing motionless on the shore while I'm drowning.

RODEZ: Let's go inside.

CHINA: (*Shouting*) Alright, go in, go in, go in, go ahead, go, go inside since you have to go inside!

They look at each other frantically.

RODEZ: I have a fever, I have a fever, China, please stop hounding me.

CHINA: I have no choice, Rodez, I have already told you, I'm on fire too, but remember. Remember that it was you. You were the one who called me back, after, you called me this time on some—false—pretense, but in truth because you felt lonely, because the one-whose-life-you-shared had suddenly slipped away, you were vague on that subject, and I, as usual, I didn't ask any questions and we stayed on the telephone a long time as you told me that the one-whose-life-you-shared had abruptly vanished and you were lost. You implied that you wanted my presence, so, so of course, I ran to your rescue, well, I wasn't going to rescue you but to meet you, see you, contemplate you. My heart was beating out of my chest the whole of the journey that separated me from you. I arrived at your place. You opened your door. You were beautiful. You needed me. I sat down. I didn't know how deep I had sunk in by letting you pour your sorrow into me, I could no longer hide my disastrous transparency, I felt my forty-year-old body become heavy in front of your vigor, I. . . I dared to talk to you about us. You said some vague things, you said that the time would come, that the river always runs its course, some ridiculous things, inept, cruel, ridiculous and cruel things. I took a long walk in the street, full of the memory of you. . . That night, after the theater, I was roaming around your neighborhood, it was midnight, I called you, you told me that you would prefer it if I didn't call you so late. That is what you told me, when, a few hours before, I had rushed to your salvation, you threw that in my face and I hung up, three minutes past midnight by my watch, the cars, speeding along the boulevard and I started to cry. In the taxi that was taking me home, I said to myself that it was better for everything to be finished between us because my folly, my dissolution had no limit and then I cried myself to sleep like a teenage girl who has been cut for the first time. You feel the wind moving through the leaves?

Silence.

Rodez. . .

RODEZ: Yes...

CHINA: Rodez...

RODEZ: Yes.

CHINA: I swear to you that after that I wanted to flee, I swear it, Rodez, that I attempted to flee. Why did you call me again? Why? Tell me why.

RODEZ: I don't know why. I wanted, I admired you, I wanted for us to work together.

CHINA: Why do you keep avoiding it, why not face the brilliant, tragic fact? We were drawn toward one another like a moth to a flame. You asked me to work with you. You told me to meet you, again at your place, so that we could talk. Do you remember?

RODEZ: Yes.

CHINA: And so I went to your place, yet again, like a suicide who climbs back up ten flights of stairs to fling herself once more onto the pavement. But I thought, dare I say, I sincerely believed that I would be brave enough to tell you no, and I did in fact tell you no, I told you that I wouldn't work with you. And you asked me why. Do you remember?

RODEZ: Yes.

CHINA: And what did I tell you then?

RODEZ: I don't know.

CHINA: I told you that it was better for us not to work together, that I didn't have enough resistance within me to face your presence every day, and you—murderer—pretended that you didn't understand, you kept insisting that this meeting was a simple transaction and you blamed me for withholding. But I wasn't withholding, Rodez, I was saying plainly and freely that I was broken, sunk, and that in order to—keep from dying, I had to distance myself from you, go on and tell me that wasn't what I said, I dare you. I told you that, Rodez. Didn't I?

RODEZ: Yes.

CHINA: Why didn't I leave at that very moment, thick with my sadness, with the futility of everything, thick with forty useless years of searching for you, years that led me painfully to you, in an exhausting pilgrimage at the end of which I had to backtrack through the ruts, return at dusk, to loneliness, to the drying up of my self and my beauty? It must have been because—after you had plunged in the first spears—I wanted you to deliver the fatal blow and I offered myself up, perpetually still, how can I tell you? how can I describe my incredible awareness of that moment, even while I stood apart from it and, calm, clear, a stranger to myself, emptied of my guts, I saw myself falling endlessly without ever crashing down to that sea which would have taken me into its definitive immensity. But you—criminal—you clenched me in the grip of your smiles and your hatred, because you hated me, Rodez, at that very moment you hated me, because at that very moment I kept myself from you, you were no longer the one who could slip, smooth and polished, from my grasp, but it was me, or rather a part of myself that was escaping the jaws of your. . .

And yet, and yet we went out together, into the light and, as in a dream, like one administers a drug, a poison, you invited me to lunch, and as in a dream, I heard myself say yes and I saw myself seated at the table across from you in that Indian restaurant, do you remember?

RODEZ: Yes.

CHINA: I was watching you sitting there and watching you, I understood that you had to be alive because you were hungry, because you had a strength in you that I no longer possessed, a strength that let you send a dish back because it wasn't good, order something else and eat it in front of me. . . oh, my god, my god, my god, my god! Step out of the ring. Run away. Flee. Run away, I should have, I should have fled.

We hear the sea.

> When I took you in my mouth. It happened at your place, yes, again at your place, because after the restaurant we went back to your apartment, I don't know what made me go there, anyway, I, we stayed for a long time next to one another. You put some music on. I got up, I went over and stroked your shoulder. You told me you didn't want me to caress you. So I stood still. No one said anything. I put on my summer coat. You and me at the door. I was looking at you and you wouldn't look at me and I couldn't help but think of the two of us a few weeks before. You opened the door and I took a step out into the silence and then suddenly, I don't know why, don't ask me why, I closed the door, I took off the coat which fell to the floor without a sound and I started to caress you. You were saying no, you were telling me to stop, not to caress you, but I kept on, I unbuttoned your shirt, stroked your chest, your stomach, and you kept murmuring unintelligible supplications, while I undressed you. And then I took you in my mouth and I held it a long time, you tasted of salt, you were still, like a statue, up against the wall, silent, undone, and a few seconds later, I don't know how, don't ask me how, we were on your bed, in your bedroom, and I finished undressing you. How long did I stay there caressing you? You made no movement whatsoever, your gaze was elsewhere, oh far away, full of emptiness and fog, and pained. My face was close to yours, I wanted to plunge my eyes into yours, my mouth into your mouth, but you were looking so much further off, and you refused my lips. Then, as in a dream, burnt alive, I got up, I left you lying there, naked, on your bed, I walked in silence, I put on my coat, I went down the stairs and then all of a sudden I found myself once again like in one of those recurring nightmares, in front of your building, in the light. I walked back down the street and then I don't know. I don't know anymore. Rodez. . .

Silence.

> Rodez. Rodez. Rodez. Rodez, I'm going to have to tell you. . . what you already know but. . . what I had promised myself never to say, what I was keeping hidden in the bottom of my guts but now it's coming back to the surface, dense, endless and sweet,

like a sacred spit, ah!, Rodez, I have to tell you that I loved you, that I loved you, that I loved you, that I. . . There are no other words, I, no other words, loved you, I loved you, I loved you, I loved you, I loved you, Rodez, forgive me, forgive, I beg you to forgive me, tonight I give up, I surrender, lifeless, powerless, defenseless, powerless, defenseless, lifeless, vanquished, defeated, forgive me, I'm saying it, the obscene, I'm saying it, the bitter cold of unrequited love, the disaster, I loved you, Rodez, I loved you, I loved you—do you understand?—there are no other words, I loved you, there are no other words, those are the only words, no others, Rodez! there is nothing else, no other words.

Silence. She sobs for a long time.

All of my body's tears. My sight is clouded. A widow's veil over my pupils. Close the eyelids so as not to be blinded by you. Dream of infinity. They talk about a Christmas truce. I would like for you to come closer to me. I would like for you not to be afraid anymore. You feel the wind in the leaves, the smell of the sea, bewitching, gray tonight in the throes of its foaming, shameless, sparkling, abandoned, a hindrance to its own motion, unrelenting and repetitive? I love you, Rodez. I have loved you. (*Silence*) Did you get the roses?

A few days later I left. That friend came with me. We left the city. A limpid sky, not a cloud, harsh sun softened by the wind. I had sent you roses. Did you get the roses, with those lines by Aragon. . .?

RODEZ: "It is easier to die than to love."

CHINA: I stayed alone, for a long time, in that house, with the sound of the sea, with no echo inside me.

The sound of the music from inside. They fall silent.

I heard about the accident. Who told me? How did I find out? Why have me informed? I called you. Your voice, calm, on the telephone. . . You told me that one of your friends had been killed in the accident. You told me that, and you told me that you were unharmed, only your right hand had. . .

The music again, jolting, captivating. They look at each other. Slowly their bodies meet. They dance, imperceptibly, without even touching. Little by little the dance becomes more intimate, their legs intertwine, gently, to the rhythm. Pressed against one another, they sway. Their hips locked, moving, in a slow, exasperated desire. She tries to kiss him. He refuses or gives in. He finally gets away, begins to sob, collapses, sinks to the ground.

Stand up.

Silence.

Please. Stand up.

Silence.

RODEZ: No. No. . . No. No. No. No. No. Ah. That sky, swaying above the. . . it's all, it's all dark above the. . . It's all, it's all black. . . they're dancing inside, the sweat, been dancing all night—you hear them dancing, China?—a ship that pitches and keeps pushing along, crushing the swell. No. No. Ah. Leave me. Alone. I have a fever. Did I tell you that I have a fever? Dawn is here, ready to break and I'm asking for a reprieve, give me one more piece of darkness. I'm not well. I am not well. I have always hated Christmas, the Christmas truce as you said, and even in the heat of our country, tonight, I can't stand Christmas Eve. Don't say anything, let me finish. Now here I am, with the vastness of this sky, of this ocean that makes me sick, as my only horizon, and I can go neither forward nor back, too tired to return to the crowd and the bodies stuck together in their desire. I am not well, China. Do you understand? How did you know I was here? Who told you? By what uncontrollable fate did you find yourself here in front of me with that dress around your body and those pearls wrapped on your neck. . . Migratory birds. . . I thought you were thousands of miles away from me. I thought you were in France, on stage. Let me finish. I saw you, you had your back to me, I was watching the dancers move and I saw you. Then you were swallowed by the mass of bodies and. . . I can't remember. . . I forgot what I wanted to say. . . a gentle sob like our rainstorms, warm. It doesn't matter. . . Someone leaned over to me but I didn't hear what he was whispering in my ear because the music was drowning out all the sound. Then, then I spotted you again, dancing in the middle of the crowd, lewd, attached to that stranger, clutching him furiously to keep from sinking. I said to myself it would be better for you and for me if I left before you noticed I was here. But I couldn't. Because I couldn't anymore. We had by some—immeasurable—chance washed up, both of us, in this night club by the ocean, thousands of miles from France, in the middle of a long night. I saw you again in the sea, I mean in the crowd, you were dancing with a different man, you were haughty, distant, indifferent to everything, focused on your secret and suddenly your gaze pitched over toward me and you stopped. You stood still in the midst of the crowd and all you did was look at me. You came over to me, there you were in front of me, with that black dress, flowing around your body like a robe of light and you asked me if I had received your roses. (*Silence*). Of course. A thousand roses, China. (*He weeps*) You sent me a thousand roses. How can you reply to a woman who sends you a thousand roses? What can you say to a woman who one day sent you a thousand roses?

He gets up. Silence. The sound of the music.

What was. . . what was I saying? I. . . Yes. I also left the next day after that. (*Silence*) A friend came with me. I remember that day too—how did you put it?—yes, a limpid sky, not a cloud, harsh sun softened by the wind, the already faded colors of the end of a French summer, quiet fields as far as the eye can see and then the accident. . . What about it? What is there to say? What can I. . . There's nothing to. . . I have no memory of it. I woke up in a room, I had a few bruises and a deep cut on my right hand and they told me that the one-whose-life-I-shared had been killed. Yes. (*Silence*) I didn't react. Numbed, you understand? I looked at my hand, the bandage a blinding white. There. That's all. That's. . . Yes. . . Don't. . . don't say anything. . . When I went home, I was walking slowly, carried by fatigue, and. . . I found the thousand red roses. The building manager had left them in front of my door. They had withered. A thousand withered roses. Everything is so ludicrous. Isn't it? Don't you find it all ludicrous?

Are you cold?

CHINA: Dizzy.

RODEZ: Yes. (*Silence*) "It is easier to die than to love. . ."

CHINA: . . . "That is why I take the trouble to live. . ."

RODEZ: ". . . my love." Yes. (*Silence*) I don't know, China, I don't know. I don't know anymore. You've left me nothing. Only the husk. You see. Again tonight I followed you out onto this terrace. And you stole my night from me. You're probably right. You're probably right, China. But in the end, what does it matter. I, honestly, I don't see how any of that matters anymore. If the sun could just not come up, all of that would surely have some meaning, but because the sun is coming up, because dawn is here, all of that is only sound and fury, fading away, because now we must face that glimmer over there and this long day that must be gotten through, from start to finish, and then probably others, broken up by nights. It's true that we are alike, China, drawn toward one another like a moth to a flame, but is that a reason to. . . God, I am so tired, you are so pale in this growing light of day and god, I have nothing to say to you, in any case nothing to add to what you have already said! My hand hurts and I can't catch my breath. This sudden freshness, we could almost be in France, all of a sudden. Look at the sky, China, so still, let's take the time, because it's dawn, because we will have to face the day, let's take the time to look at this sky trembling in front of us. I'm not well, China. I don't feel very. . . (*Silence*) You are beautiful. (*Silence*) Please. Let's stay here, please, together or apart. Whichever you like. Let's stay here. Because now, startled by the daylight, struck through by the wind, we no longer have the strength to move. Let's stay here, China. You and me. Let's stay here and look at the day as we can't help but look at the day. Don't cry. Don't cry. Don't cry, China. Don't cry. Please. Please. Please. China, don't cry. China . . . China . . . Will you stay next to me for a moment, still?

AND THE WHOLE WORLD QUAKES: CHRONICLE OF A SLAUGHTER FORETOLD
by
Guy Régis Jr

HAITI

translation by Judith Miller

For my young brother Etzer, and for all the dead who remain unburied

A Prefatory Remark

At the same time that Haiti suffered the worst humanitarian catastrophe ever recorded, two nations, France and the U.S.A., among the dozens of others who had come to bring aid to a helpless population—which is why so many had come—started their own small war. A battle whose *raison d'être* was absolutely frivolous given the horrendous situation they were meant to come to grips with. Scrapping and yelping, the French and Americans started quarreling over the landing strip at the airport, whose buildings—the terminal and especially the control tower—had been seriously damaged. Thus was undermined the entire process of putting into place international aid. This text, which is a fiction and far from being an exact witnessing of what happened, is, nevertheless, an act of accusation. An accusation against the international community's response of total indifference to the frivolous quarrel—registering as a lack of solidarity with the traumatized country it had supposedly come to help.

Guy Régis Jr

VANOX: What time is it?
STEPHANO: According to the moon, it must be midnight.

> Maurice Maeterlinck, *Princess Maleine*

Translator's Note:

This play, a meditation, a lament, a cry of rage, and an exorcism after the 2010 earthquake that devastated many parts of Haiti and killed over 300,000 people, should be understood as a dreamscape (or, rather, a nightmare). Its allegorical nature should be obvious. Yet, its rootedness in Haitian culture is also signaled by the Creole spoken by the characters. I have kept the Creole in the text, so that it can be performed as integral to the play's lyricism. If, however, this is not possible, a translation of the lines in Creole can be found at the end of the play.

Characters:

YOUNG WOMAN (also known as "The YOUNG ONE")

OLDER WOMAN (also known as "The OLDEST")

Neon Sign: *Omnia Mors Aequat* ("Death makes everyone equal.")

SETTING

A thousand-year old tree, a giant—planted in the earth as if defying humankind, standing tall, its verticality persisting, despite everything else having fallen. A supremely starry sky—its infinite stretch, its emptiness impossible to fill, a sign of the human condition. Shooting stars—metaphysics, the transmigration of souls, and spirits. A neon sign, with the words: "Omnia Mors Aequat." Of all these elements, none of which is real or absolutely indispensable, it is the sense of collapse that must remain central, collapse being the most important feeling emanating from the stage at the play's opening.

A plaintive chant, sung by a multitude of voices, fills the night. Long silence. Then. . .

YOUNG WOMAN: Hey! Hey!

OLDER WOMAN: Yeah?

YOUNG WOMAN: Hey! Are you sleeping?

OLDER WOMAN: Yeah. Yeah!

Pause. Blackout.

YOUNG WOMAN: Hey! Hey! Hey!

OLDER WOMAN: Yeah?

YOUNG WOMAN:. . . ?

OLDER WOMAN: Yeah?

YOUNG WOMAN: You're sleeping. Aren't you?

OLDER WOMAN: No.

Pause. Blackout.

YOUNG WOMAN: No? Look. Please look then. Look! Touch me.

OLDER WOMAN: Yeah? What?

YOUNG WOMAN: Touch me. It's important. Can you feel my blood beating in your hand? Touch. Do you feel it?

OLDER WOMAN: (*Without emotion*) Yeah, yeah!

YOUNG WOMAN: (*Upset*) You're still sleeping.

OLDER WOMAN: No, I'm not sleeping.

YOUNG WOMAN: So we can start again?

Pause. Blackout.

OLDER WOMAN: (*Asking herself*) What time is it?

YOUNG WOMAN: (*Same kind of question*) What time is it?

OLDER WOMAN: What time could it be?

Pause. Blackout.

YOUNG WOMAN: Are you sleeping now? No? So whatever time it is, can we start our game again, begin over?

OLDER WOMAN: No.

YOUNG WOMAN: But we can't do what they're doing. Those slackers. They chant the whole night long, they pray, they implore, they hug the earth with their faces. . . And I've come back. I'm back again. . . Now it's stopped. Their lamentations. Their chants. Ignoring everything that's been happening, everything about those foreigners, those missionaries who're taking advantage of the situation to invade us, who're profiting from our paralysis. Those hysterics who've come to save us, and make us pay. . . They don't even see the beautiful sky over our heads. Even this beautiful sky right here. Yes, always praying, always complaining bitterly when everything's going wrong, when they're in a hole, when everything falls on top of them. It's always the others who must come and save us. . . We ought to get up. Now that they've shut up, we can start again. Are you sleeping?

OLDER WOMAN: No. Who can? Who? It'll never be the way it was. It can never be the same again. Never the same. Never. *Pèsòn pa ka dòmi! Pèsòn, pèsòn moun pa ka dòmi kè poze, repoze! Pèsòn! Menm si yo ta vle, pèsòn! Pèsòn pas ka fouti dòmi ankò! Randevou kase. Men, pa gen lè. Li ka pwente, vini, lè li vle, san zatann. Ankenn moun pa dwe dòmi. Ki ès ki ta swete file desann tankou zèklè nan syèl, mouri tèt nwè?*[1] Who wants to melt into the depths of the night, whoosh, disappear? There have already been so many, so many who've slipped away. *Veye! Oui, veye! Rete la! Veye nou tout! Je* *klè!*² An eye. Always one. One eye to see. One eye opened wide. Even if there's nothing we can do. At least one. Yes, one. Because we don't know, we can't know when that thing will show up, come back to crush everything, finish us off. We don't know. Who can? Who can know? Who can tell us? Who? Nobody, nobody will sleep again the sleep of the just. Yes, that! Yes, the sweet and restful sleep we deserve. We don't sleep that good sleep. No. We don't sleep. *En, ki ès ki ka fèmen je li pou li dòmi?*³ No, no one has slept since. Me, neither, I don't sleep. I sleep a little—but I don't sleep. . . Look! One! Look! *Gade, gade! Yon zetwal!*⁴ One—one slicing through the great stretch of sky and falling, disappearing! Two! I saw another one while that one was disappearing—falling and falling. Two shooting stars, bleeding into the sky, peacefully. Two stars in the night. Dazzling.

YOUNG WOMAN: Yes! Two!

OLDER WOMAN: *Dat nou la nou ap veye. Chak jou nou de, blayi, espanta, san rezon! Mwen ta renmen poze tèt mwen dòmi! Mwen ta renmen fin pa poze tèt mwne repoze, men mwen rete la tennfas, mwen ap veye. Mwen ta renmen rive soupi yon ti kras. Mwen tou, dòmi anpe alafen. O! Soupi kò mwen! Lonje kòm dòmi! Men mwen pa rive dòmi. Mwen pa rive. Mwne pa ka. Menm si kòm febli, anyen mwen pa ka.*⁵

YOUNG WOMAN: You can't. How could you? You're right. You can't. We can't. Impossible.

OLDER WOMAN: Another one, look.

YOUNG WOMAN: Another one?

OLDER WOMAN: Yes. One, over there. Do you see it? Look, look, look. It's sliding, slipping. Follow it with your eyes, follow it. [*sings*] *File zetwal! File!*⁶. . . Where were you?

YOUNG WOMAN: I was there, over there, leaning against the other side of the tree, on another part. Watching the city below us—extinguished. Missionaries, foreigners, deciding what works and what doesn't. They're taking charge, burrowing everywhere.

OLDER WOMAN: *Konte Zetwal. Pou kisa? Sa nou konte fè? Zetwal tonbe, sa nou konte fè? Pou ki nap pèdi tèt nou konte? Pouki nou konte fè? Sa n'ap konte fè?*[7]

Pause.

Ou pa di anyen? Sa nou ka fè ak sa?[8]

YOUNG WOMAN: *Sa nou ka fè!*[9]

OLDER WOMAN: *Ton lòt ankò! Gade, gade, gade*! Another one, yes. *Gade, gade, gade, gade, gade!*[10] Again!

YOUNG WOMAN: One more.

OLDER WOMAN: One more, yes!

YOUNG WOMAN: I see. How many will it take to close this chapter? It's crazy to count like this. It'll take too much time. Yes, crazy to count all those sparks, all that snuffing out. All those passages, all that slipping, shooting, and sliding. We'll never finish.

OLDER WOMAN: No. We can't stop. We can't stop our game. Now that we've begun, this game is infinite; we have to keep on, begin again, each time. You can't stop. You can't. Yes, let's keep on counting, enumerating, voicing the numbers. It's not a waste of time. All those people really counted for us. You know they did. . . So, we have to keep on counting. Yes. Our long-haul game. Our endless ritual. Then, we'll sleep. When we'll be finished, we'll have all the time in the world to sleep—after.

YOUNG WOMAN: Do you believe that? We'll be able to sleep, finally? You believe it? Really, you believe it? After all this?

OLDER WOMAN: Yes, it will calm us. We'll be calm after. So, we'll sleep.

YOUNG WOMAN: (*She sighs*) At last!

OLDER WOMAN: What, at last? Why that big sigh?

YOUNG WOMAN: (*Asking herself*) What time is it?

OLDER WOMAN: Time? I don't know.

YOUNG WOMAN: Touch me.

Pause.

You have nothing to say?

OLDER WOMAN: What?

YOUNG WOMAN: Touch my body.

OLDER WOMAN: Another one!

YOUNG WOMAN: No.

OLDER WOMAN: Yes. Another!

YOUNG WOMAN: No, not even the speck of another, not one. Not the least trace of another star. I don't see it. There's nothing in this sky. Nothing.

OLDER WOMAN: Am I losing my mind? Am I making all this up? I saw something. I did. Don't you see?

YOUNG WOMAN: Touch me. Please touch me.

OLDER WOMAN: No. Look, over there! Right over there, in that other quadrant. Don't you see that one? Don't you see? Look, look, look.

YOUNG ONE: Yes, yes, this time.

OLDER WOMAN: Yes, count. Go ahead. Instead of pitying ourselves, let's calculate, let's count those who count for us.

YOUNG ONE: (*Overwhelmed*) How long will this last? Huh? Yes? Yes?

OLDER ONE: (*In a daze*) Huh? I don't know. All those people? I don't know.

YOUNG WOMAN: (*She sighs*) Yeah!

OLDER WOMAN: (*She sighs too*) Yeah! Big sigh! Yeah! Big sigh!

Beat.

YOUNG WOMAN: (*Angry, vengeful*) And those who come, they're arriving by the thousands. All those thousands of coalitions, of countries. They're organized, they're everywhere. All of them, those foreigners. Nation against nation—in order to invade us, install themselves, take their places, stay. Despite the shipwreck. They don't give a damn about our distress. They're only sad, suddenly, when they have to defend their own position on our land. They don't even have time to ask if we see them, if we see them with our own two eyes—us too. Don't you see them? Haven't you seen them? How they're fighting each other! Right in front of our eyes, our own two eyes, they're tearing each other to pieces, fighting for their position. Each one with their coalition, their uniform, their army. They're plotting their invasion. All that for us.

OLDER WOMAN: For us? You see!

YOUNG WOMAN: We shouldn't give a shit about their quarrel. We shouldn't. We didn't ask for anything.

OLDER WOMAN: But they feel sorry for us, for what happened to us. World-wide solidarity—international pity.

YOUNG WOMAN: We don't want their pity.

OLDER WOMAN: (*Ironically*) They're traumatized.

YOUNG WOMAN: What can we do about it?

OLDER WOMAN: They're bringing us help. We are. . . important, important to them. . . capital.

YOUNG WOMAN: Capital, right, capital!

OLDER WOMAN: Anyway, they're here. And us—we can't do a thing about it. They're here, taking their places on the request of our leaders, who summoned them—our leaders.

YOUNG WOMAN: Our leaders? What leaders?

OLDER WOMAN: The country's.

YOUNG WOMAN: Them? Always waiting for the Messiah? For somebody to come and save them? And what country? There is no country. There is no country any more. What country are you talking about? You're joking. What country?

OLDER WOMAN: I don't know.

YOUNG WOMAN: Yes. They won't leave. What are they really doing here?

OLDER WOMAN: They're analyzing our situation. There're even some among them—specialists—taking notes, summing things up; they want to help. Can you see them? I don't see them. Do you?

YOUNG WOMAN: I don't see them either. I see them, but I don't see them.

OLDER WOMAN: What are you saying? Are you laughing? What are you saying?

YOUNG WOMAN: No. Nothing. I'm not laughing. I'm joking, like you. I'm joking. That's all. I didn't say anything. Anyhow, it's all our fault. A dead body attracts flies.

OLDER WOMAN: But?

YOUNG WOMAN: I'm telling you I don't see them. That's all.

OLDER WOMAN: (*Ironic*) And there are those who are leaving. Them—they're leaving in the thousands.

YOUNG WOMAN: (*Also ironic*) Those who can.

OLDER WOMAN: (*Same emphasis*) They're leaving us behind.

YOUNG WOMAN: They're saving themselves. Foreigners are showing up. Our people are leaving.

OLDER WOMAN: They're going far away; they won't come back.

YOUNG WOMAN: How can you be so sure?

OLDER WOMAN: They were already leaving us, leaving us behind. It doesn't date from today. Thousands of them were already leaving us.

YOUNG WOMAN: Ah. . .

OLDER WOMAN: You see?

YOUNG WOMAN: Yes.

OLDER WOMAN: None of that is so new—the comings and goings of catastrophes and people. We're pretty used to it. Coalitions, catastrophes that come, that go. Their dance, their endless puppet show.

YOUNG WOMAN: (*Laughs*) You mean, we already know misfortune and it's already well acquainted with us!

OLDER WOMAN: What are you saying, are you at it again? You're laughing? You think you can laugh about it?

YOUNG WOMAN: (*Laughs*) What? No. I'm not laughing. . . Well. I am laughing about it. Sometimes I have to, I confess. And you? You too?

OLDER WOMAN: (*With emphasis*) Yes. . .

YOUNG WOMAN: (*With emphasis*) Yes. . .

OLDER WOMAN: You were saying?

YOUNG WOMAN: It was you: yes. . .

OLDER WOMAN: You drive me crazy. (*Asking herself*) What time is it?

YOUNG WOMAN: Time to start up again. To begin again. Let's do it. Let's play our game. Let's take our positions. Only way to laugh about it. Only way. Laugh with evil. Exorcize it. Let's go!

OLDER WOMAN: (*Annoyed*) What time is it?... Why? You're the one who stopped everything. You went away? It was you, wasn't it?

YOUNG WOMAN: But I came back. I'm here now.

OLDER WOMAN: (*Even more annoyed*) What time is it?

YOUNG WOMAN: Why?

OLDER WOMAN: Why did you go away, leave me? I was afraid you'd disappeared for good, afraid you were running away from me. What time is it?

YOUNG WOMAN: I don't know. . . I was here. I wasn't going anywhere.

Pause.

(*Evasive*) What were we talking about?

OLDER WOMAN: About those who leave, who abandon the country, leaving us behind with our misery. We were talking about those who leave us.

YOUNG WOMAN: And so what? It's their right.

OLDER WOMAN: Yes. But what about us? We just stay here. . . Who cares? Let them leave, run away—if they can. Far, very far, very far from us, let them.

YOUNG WOMAN: It's strange. Those comings and goings. Don't you think? It's strange all the same. Those who go, who come. And that international solidarity. Yeah. Them. What right do they have to come and treat us the way they do—this whole world of people? Us—the part of the world they have to save. A priority zone. What are they afraid of? Why don't they huddle together in their good fortune? Why all of a sudden such interest in us, such a need to wipe their conscience clean? With their summing up, their reporting. Why? Instead of keeping busy with something else. . . Rather than filming us in our disarray. Rather than watching us survive, for better and for worse, for better and for worse, yes, for better and for worse.

OLDER WOMAN: (*Laughs, irony*) We move them.

YOUNG WOMAN: They're moved, and us—we can't hide any more. They cage us, stigmatize us. That's how it is. All our suffering exhibited right in their faces; they stigmatize us. That's all we are in their eyes.

OLDER WOMAN: (*Emphatically*) That's right.

YOUNG WOMAN: So now's the time for them to come and dig in. The right moment. Never hesitating to tell us what we should do. Long lessons on how to behave, how to learn, how to imitate them, imitate what they do. They'll never stop plotting. They'll come, dig in, set up their barracks, their campsites for all eternity—and adopt us.

OLDER WOMAN: (*Same emotion*) That's right.

YOUNG WOMAN: Let them come. What can we do? If they have nothing fucking better? What can we do? Let them come! That's the way it is. What the fuck does it matter? Let them do their thing, accomplish their mission, their great mission—on our backs. Their timeless crusade. Those missionaries.

OLDER WOMAN: As long as we're as low as possible in their esteem, they might as well come, take advantage of the situation. That's right. Let them come. Let them come take care of us, of our misery, prolong the occupation. Let's hope it does them good. We can hope they get a big prize. Anyhow, it's done. We can't get along without them. If they come, it's to stay. Until they find other things to do, other places to invade, to gift with their solutions to misfortune. After all, that's their job. Misfortune is their prey. No. Let them be. We hope our misfortune will feed them well—those opportunists—bring them lots of money.

YOUNG WOMAN: *Ala tris sa en! Ala sa tris sa, en!*[11]

OLDER WOMAN: *Ala wont!*[12]

YOUNG WOMAN: *Ala tris! Ala tris!*[13] A star, look!

OLDER WOMAN: You saw it? You saw it too? Did you really see it as I saw it, shooting—like that, whoosh, you saw it?

YOUNG WOMAN: A star, yes.

OLDER WOMAN: Yeah, yeah!

YOUNG WOMAN: What are we going to do now? Now that we have nothing to do, what are we going to invent? Have you thought about it?

OLDER WOMAN: No.

YOUNG WOMAN: No?

OLDER WOMAN: I don't see anything.

YOUNG WOMAN: She doesn't see anything. Nothing.

OLDER WOMAN: You?

YOUNG WOMAN: Me?

OLDER WOMAN: Yes, you.

YOUNG WOMAN: Why? Me? Me neither. Nothing. Yes, you're right. What I see is: we stay rooted here, yes, we stay rooted here, rooted in order to number, to count the stars, the only thing to do. That's it then? *Ala tris!*

OLDER WOMAN: *Ala en!*[14]

YOUNG WOMAN: Oh! Oh! Oh! Oh! Oh! Oh!

OLDER WOMAN: *Ala en!*

YOUNG WOMAN: (*Overwhelmed*) Not another word. Not another thought. What I see is the great collapse.

OLDER WOMAN: (*Dazed*) Yeah.

YOUNG WOMAN: Right, huh? The great collapse.

OLDER WOMAN: Yes!

YOUNG WOMAN: Yes, right? Yes?

OLDER WOMAN: Yes!

YOUNG WOMAN: Yes?

OLDER WOMAN: Yes!

YOUNG WOMAN: Yes?

OLDER WOMAN: Yes!

YOUNG WOMAN: Yes, right? Yes?

OLDER WOMAN: Yes, yes, yes.

YOUNG WOMAN: Yes!

OLDER WOMAN: Yes!

YOUNG WOMAN: Yes, yes, yes. The great collapse.

Pause.

But you—say something, speak, say anything, anything, speak. That's it, speak, I'm waiting for you, I'm counting on you, you're what I'm counting on. You must have an idea? What are we supposed to do? How can we do anything? How? We can't decide to simply stay here? You and me? You know it.

OLDER WOMAN: Yes, I know it.

YOUNG WOMAN: Couldn't we just be happy to live, to breathe? Couldn't we?

OLDER WOMAN: No. We couldn't.

YOUNG WOMAN: So what are we going to do?

OLDER WOMAN: I don't know. I don't know. Please. I don't know. Please. Stop. Please.

Pause.

YOUNG WOMAN: Just don't give up. Don't cry. I'm wrecked too. But don't give up.

Beat.

OLDER WOMAN: Maybe we could sell? Like other women—sell, do some business, sell small things. They do that. Everybody sells. To fool their misery, like they say, they sell.

YOUNG WOMAN: What?

OLDER WOMAN: Things, small things.

YOUNG WOMAN: We don't know how. It won't work. We don't know how. (*Laughs, to herself*) We don't know how to sell anything else.

OLDER WOMAN: You're laughing? Aren't you? You're laughing about it? That's not how we'll get out of this. You laugh. And what about those lofty words? I thought you wanted us to change? You wanted another life. Done with the one you had before. Finished—that depraved life. Isn't that what you said?

YOUNG WOMAN: Yes. I said that. I know. But now that he's. . . that he's not here, not alive. . . no, I don't want that life, not any more. (*Overwhelmed*) *A, sak ta di sa? Ayayay! Sa k ta di sa en?*[15]

OLDER WOMAN: *Kisa?*[16]

YOUNG WOMAN: *Ou pa konprenn?*[17] Don't tell me you don't understand?

OLDER WOMAN: No.

YOUNG WOMAN: *Bèl Amou!? Bèl Amou tonbe!? Bèl Amou tonbe!? Bèl Amou* no longer exists. He's dead. *Bèl Amou tonbe, pfft. O! Bèl Amou tonbe. Bèl Amou tonbe.*

OLDER WOMAN: Yes, like so many others. So many others. A huge number in fact. Why?

YOUNG WOMAN: Don't tell me. . . No, don't tell me it means nothing to you? Don't tell me that.

OLDER WOMAN: So, *Bèl Amou tonbe.*

YOUNG WOMAN: Maybe you're not shocked. But I didn't see it like that. I didn't see him so fragile, so vulnerable. I didn't see it.

OLDER WOMAN: But there it is. Like that.

YOUNG WOMAN: *E nou? Sa nou ka fè?*[18]

OLDER WOMAN: We'll find something.

YOUNG WOMAN: They're all dead. All of them. All our clients. All of them.

OLDER WOMAN: Yes, there's nobody left—hardly anyone. There's not a thing left either. On the boulevard, the old boulevard, where Bèl Amou's place used to be, that great big boulevard Jean-Jacques

Dessalines, the main street, you saw it, nothing's standing. There's nothing left.

YOUNG WOMAN: Yes.

OLD WOMAN: Nothing we know is left standing. No, nothing we know. There's nothing there. But we'll find something. We'll find something.

YOUNG WOMAN: Tell me. Yes? Tell me. It's impossible. Impossible—all that. What's happened is impossible. Tell me. Yes?

OLDER WOMAN: What?

YOUNG WOMAN: Tell me.

OLDER WOMAN: What?

YOUNG WOMAN: Tell me.

OLDER WOMAN: I ask myself too. Ask myself. What happened? No explanation. What happened to make everything fall? In just a few seconds, that huge implosion, with all those people? No, there's nothing to say. Nothing, I'm telling you. What did they call it? The great collapse. Everywhere.

YOUNG WOMAN: Yes, for the whole world. And the whole world quakes from our great collapse.

OLDER WOMAN: Yeah! Yeah! Yeah! Yeah! Yeah! Yeah!

YOUNG WOMAN: *Pe! Pe!*[19]

OLDER WOMAN: Yeah. Let's shut up!

YOUNG WOMAN: We've already shut up. We don't speak any more. We don't speak. We've already shut ourselves up. We already shut up. We speak a little, but we don't speak.

OLDER WOMAN: Yes. It's true. It's true.

YOUNG WOMAN: Ah! *Bèl Amou tonbe! Bèl Amou tonbe vre! Bèl Amou tonbe!* How are we going to take care of ourselves? What can we do?

OLDER WOMAN: Think, think for ourselves. Even if now, now at this moment, we still can't think.

YOUNG WOMAN: That's true too.

OLDER WOMAN: Yes, for us. And not far away, not far away—you can count, make a long list. We're not the only ones. Plenty of others have empty lives.

YOUNG WOMAN: Yes. It's true.

OLDER WOMAN: We should be thankful. We should thank the heavens—somebody—that we're still here, speaking. Everything fell, but we're still alive, alive and well, right? We can touch each other, prove it.

YOUNG WOMAN: (*Overwhelmed*) Yes?

OLDER WOMAN: (*Dazed*) Yeah. That's what I'm telling you.

YOUNG WOMAN: Yes.

OLDER WOMAN: Yes, right?

YOUNG WOMAN: Yes.

OLDER WOMAN: I know.

YOUNG WOMAN: But we have to keep on, swallow, put food in our bellies, live. Don't we?

OLDER WOMAN: Yes, right. I know.

YOUNG WOMAN: We have to keep on, that's it. We have to.

OLDER WOMAN: That's true too. It must be true.

YOUNG WOMAN: Yes!

OLDER WOMAN: Yes? Is that it? Is that it? Obligated, obligated. That's it. Like after all that torment. Doing what we're doing. We're still living. We should live better, count every day, be bold. Make each day count to deserve them.

YOUNG WOMAN: (*Suddenly in great distress*) But how?

OLDER WOMAN: We'll find a way.

YOUNG WOMAN: Yes. *Bèl Amou* was hardly paying anything. It was the end. He was hardly worth anything. Don't you know that?

OLDER WOMAN: Yes. I know it. We all knew it. But!

YOUNG WOMAN: Yes, that's the thing: But! That's the thing. He was useful. We had to. . . we could manage with him. Even if he wasn't much good, wasn't worth anything anymore. He was finished. He didn't count any more. The end of a reign, end of a life. Then, that thing, that avalanche, that horrible catastrophe. . . What did they call it? Those journalists? They had a way of naming it. . . The slaughter.

OLDER WOMAN: The Apocalypse in our Lifetime.

YOUNG WOMAN: That's it, exactly. The Apocalypse.

OLDER WOMAN: So atrocious!

YOUNG WOMAN: Who are you talking about? Them? Him?

OLDER WOMAN: No. The journalists. Yes. Him too. I would've wanted him to hold on, like us, at least see this, him too. I would have wanted him to watch his fall with his own eyes, his miserly ending, drop by drop. He who was expecting a quiet death. I would have wanted a longer death for him. A long, long infinite decline. Like the way an old lion yawns in his cage, waiting for the inevitable end—so debonair.

Pause.

YOUNG WOMAN: Don't cry.

OLDER WOMAN: I'm not crying. No.

Beat.

> You're the one. You're the one crying. Dry your tears, I'm telling you. Don't cry. You shouldn't give him that gift. You shouldn't be so touched by him. Look. I'm not crying. Almost, but I'm not. We can't. We can't let him take pleasure in our sadness—after. Not him. We won't cry, OK? We shouldn't cry for him. What good does it do? Tell me.

YOUNG WOMAN: Yes, right? What good?

OLDER WOMAN: I know. I haven't stopped. His fate. . . I haven't stopped.

YOUNG WOMAN: Yes, right? Me neither. But let's stop now! We have to stand up. The other girls would be ashamed of us. The others. The girls. Yes, huh?

OLDER WOMAN: Yes, it's true. You're right. We should dry them up. It's over.

YOUNG WOMAN: Dry them up?

OLDER WOMAN: Our eyes, we need to dry them, look things right in the face.

YOUNG WOMAN: Yes, let's stop! Let's not cry. We can't. We mustn't. Not for him.

OLDER WOMAN: No, Yes, right? Yes? Yes. You're right. . . But I never see, I never see it coming. And I can't stop it from coming. I cry, that's all. When it comes, I cry, I cry, that's all. Yes, you know?

YOUNG WOMAN: Me too. But just the same, we have to stop. Find a reason to dry our eyes, like you say. From now on, stop everything, dry our eyes, and look at what life can be like—after. In front of us, everything is in front of us now. After the apocalypse—everything. We should be proud to have had that luck. We should. Of so many others, here we are, us two—alone. Another chance at life. To start over. To begin again.

OLDER WOMAN: Yes, start over.

YOUNG WOMAN: *Tabula Rasa*!

OLDER WOMAN: Start over, at zero, yes, begin again.

YOUNG WOMAN: Yes, *Tabula Rasa*! Make our destiny something we deserve.

OLDER WOMAN: That's beautiful. What you're saying is beautiful. Where do you find the strength to say such things, to be so sure. It's beautiful, really beautiful!

YOUNG WOMAN: Abandon that dangerous life. No longer be the woman every kind of crook, every bandit embarks—and then mounts. No longer their slave. Live, live, live—finally. And make babies, lots of babies, lots.

OLDER WOMAN: Yes, huh? We have to live no matter what, make a life. Forget our beautiful whorehouse, its ending in ashes. Our *Bèl Amou*!

YOUNG WOMAN: Babies. Lots of them.

OLDER WOMAN: Are you sure? We have to live, yes, no matter what—live, grab onto life with no regrets. But should we add to it? Multiply the people out there? Should we be thinking about that now?... Oh! We're forgetting to count. We're speaking, but we've forgotten the stars.

YOUNG WOMAN: I know. But no one's saying anything, no one's up in arms about replacing—replacing the number of people who've disappeared, replacing them—after. All of them, those hundreds of thousands, and even more, the ones about to die because they're too sad, because they remember too many things. All those who've disappeared, who will disappear. Nobody's up in arms about the emptiness, the nothingness they'll leave behind, how to fill it up. It's only when we think about losing people that our heads work. Never about regeneration, renewal. It's not what you'd call glorious. . . . They count the number of people—wanting always to have fewer, to stop the growth, waiting for the next catastrophe to help out. But now? All those hundreds of thousands, how do we replace them? . . . Lots, lots, lots of babies.

OLDER WOMAN: A star. Another shooting start! Yes, *yon bèl zetwal file pou lespri anpè ak tèt li? Yon lòt ankò!*[20] You want to replace everybody all by yourself? Just you? You think you can do it?

YOUNG WOMAN: What?

OLDER WOMAN: I know. Don't pretend. I know. Do you hear me? I know.

YOUNG WOMAN: What?

Old Woman: I know what you did. I know.

YOUNG WOMAN: Who told you? Who? Was it him? Who dared? Nobody should know I did that, one last time, again. I really hate him. Why did he do it?

OLDER WOMAN: Forget it. It wasn't him. It wasn't the dead man, the one who disappeared. Nor the others either. I saw it. I knew what was going on. We all knew. And we all felt sorry, too, for your sadness, despite what you might think, might guess about us; us, too, we suffered with you. We all had the same thing happen with him. And everything about you was easy to know—you, The Young One. . . You lit up his life; he let it show.

YOUNG WOMAN: I made you all sick.

OLDER WOMAN: No. You didn't make me sick. I was jealous, but you didn't make me sick. And then, the others, they don't count anymore. Death makes us all equal.

YOUNG ONE: But even so? I know I won't have any more, not coming from me, from my womb. . . I don't need to. And then, it doesn't matter. Why should it? I won't have any more from my womb— that I know. It's me who decided. The doctor told me after this last abortion, the scraping, I risked the end, the stopping for good. I said it was an ending like any other. Like for all the others. Like for every woman when the blood stops. Childbirth. It's all our fate, isn't it? Every woman. Every woman who exists? We know that. I knew it, I did, me too. Me, too, that. . . that. . . I had the choice. I chose. It was my choice. . . That's what matters after all. I don't know. I could have. But this last one. . . I didn't want one from him either. I was just fresh meat—before another would show up, another he'd ask the same thing of, to give up having any. . . We were four, but four wasn't enough for him, despite everything. All those, those fetuses, I'm not sorry about it. I didn't want them from him. . . No. It won't be from me, that's for sure, but I will find lots now, lots. I'll find them. Replace all those others. It isn't enough for me to count, keep track of those stars, all of them. I want to be able to accomplish something, something more concrete, more regular. . . He told you his secrets, respected you, The Oldest, always needing to speak with you. And me, me, The Young One, I made sure he felt carefree, that's all. I know all that. I'm not angry with you because of it. To tell you the truth, now that we're all equal, as you say, I was jealous of you too—of everything he told you in secret. But today none of that makes any sense. Does it?

OLDER WOMAN: No. You're right. No.

YOUNG WOMAN: No?

OLDER WOMAN: No, like you say.

YOUNG WOMAN: So, then, how? How do we pick back up the normal course of things? Go down there, be with people, live with them as we used to? We can't wait like this until everything settles down. We're trapped. We're counting stars, but we're trapped. Perched up here, we're trapped.

OLDER WOMAN: Below, men are stealing, brutalizing. It's still going on. Fear, fear has invaded us, and we're here under this tree, perched, waiting for all of that to be over, be settled. Yes.

YOUNG WOMAN: I'm getting out.

OLDER WOMAN: No. Not now. Let them finish their. . . wildness. You know it, what happens, what's happening now. They take it out on women. Even with the catastrophe. Right now they're taking it out on women. Everywhere in the camps, they're taking it out on women. They're even more trapped than we are under this ancient tree. Perched, we're safe.

YOUNG WOMAN: Ha! Who says so?

OLDER WOMAN: Come on. Let them finish. Let this all pass by. They're wild now. We should hide.

YOUNG WOMAN: But does it ever stop?

OLDER WOMAN: What?

YOUNG WOMAN: You know, don't you? It never stops, the chase. You know it. War time, peace time, it's the same thing. You know it, don't you? No? No, I'm not going to stay. To wait for what? That they come here? Is that what you want?

OLDER WOMAN: I want everything to pass by. . . The sky! Look. Look. Keep yourself busy by counting. Please. Forget. Keep your mind busy. Stay busy. Count. Please count.

YOUNG WOMAN: No star. Not one. Stop. They're all dead. They might shine, but not one of them shines for us. For us they're all dead. Not one has ever shone for us. Don't you see that?

OLDER WOMAN: Look, take a minute, look.

YOUNG WOMAN: What?

OLDER WOMAN: Look.

YOUNG WOMAN: Yes, I'm looking. I'm looking, Yes.

OLDER WOMAN: Count, count now. Let's count. One, two, one hundred, one-hundred thousand.

YOUNG WOMAN: That many?

OLDER WOMAN: We need to mourn, mourn. So much snuffing out, so many disappearances. So many erasures. Yes. Yes. We must mourn. Cradle them one by one. Like a sower's hands separates the seeds, so they'll sprout and bud. Count those who're being erased, who've been erased in order to celebrate the life we still have to live—after. Please, I'm asking you. Stay. Don't go. Stay here. You matter to me. We're only two now. Only two.

YOUNG WOMAN: Yes, us, only us.

OLDER WOMAN: But you matter. You've always counted for me.

YOUNG WOMAN: Yes? I didn't know.

OLDER WOMAN: No?

YOUNG WOMAN: No.

OLDER WOMAN: You thrill me. You move me so.

YOUNG WOMAN: Me too, Yes, me too.

OLDER WOMAN: (*Surprised*) You?

YOUNG WOMAN: Yes.

OLDER WOMAN: *O, kite m touche ou. M anvi touche kò ou. Eske m ka touche kò ou on ti kras. Sèlman touche ou.*[21] Let me. Can I? Touch you. Just that. Is it OK? Touch your body.

YOUNG WOMAN: Yes.

OLDER WOMAN: How soft your body is. What are you feeling?

YOUNG WOMAN: I'm trembling. You thrill me too. It's your—your way of looking at my body. Your soft and gentle looking. Your beautiful looking, like an eagle, like the damned. Keep your hand there. Go on. Don't abandon me. Touch me. Go ahead.

OLDER WOMAN: (*She touches her and then suddenly stops, freezes.*) No. What's happening to us? What's come over us? Do you think it's the catastrophe? All this—our being together? Our fear in the mix, our hearts losing courage? Starting to crack? Do you think it's the catastrophe? . . . That if things were different. . .

YOUNG WOMAN: Touch me, I'm begging you. Come on! Don't stop now.

OLDER WOMAN: I'm sorry! I'm sorry! No.

YOUNG WOMAN: Go ahead! Go ahead! Come on!

OLDER WOMAN: Stop it!

YOUNG WOMAN: Are you OK? *ça va? ça va?* I don't get it. I don't get it, *ça va?* What's happening? I don't understand. You don't want to? Darling, are you losing your mind? You don't want to anymore?

The young woman disappears out of sight. (trans.)

OLDER WOMAN: What?

YOUNG WOMAN: I don't know.

OLDER WOMAN: Huh?

YOUNG WOMAN: Nothing. I don't know.

OLDER WOMAN: Let's drop it.

YOUNG WOMAN: I'm sorry, too.

OLDER WOMAN: Not your fault. It's me.

YOUNG WOMAN: Do I disgust you? Why? And yet I saw something in your eyes. I've seen it for a long time. I've seen it in your eyes. I know I have. . . I disgust you? Is that it?

OLDER WOMAN: Such big words. Stop it. You don't do anything to me. It's me.

YOUNG WOMAN: You? I don't understand.

OLDER WOMAN: You don't understand. I know. I would've wanted. I would've wanted so many things. So much more than this game, this ritual, this exorcism—love, love, yes, between us. Beautiful, human love. The infinite shadow of love. The love of an impossible dream. The shadow's voyage. The memory of it. Love the way you dream about it when you're little. What remains when you grow up—the shadow of this love dream. It travels within us. Love like a sweet and restful song. A sweet and restful song. A barely audible humming. But oh so restful.

> Oh, oh, oh,
> la, la, la
> la, la
> oh, oh, oh
> la, la, la
> la, la

Beat.

YOUNG WOMAN: Like that?

OLDER WOMAN: You can't understand. It's too late now.

YOUNG WOMAN: What—I don't get it. Too late? Why do you say that?

OLDER WOMAN: Are you so sure it's OK? Do you hear what I'm saying? Isn't it misfortune that's making us act like this? So different from how we would have acted—I mean at another point in time—cooler, less turbulent? Would we have acted the way we're acting now—let ourselves get carried away? I'm afraid of it. Of the energy misfortune gives us. It's wrong.

YOUNG WOMAN: And I'm afraid of your fear. I'm even more afraid of never again having enough energy to live.

OLDER WOMAN: Is that true? Come here then! Come to me! Come on!

YOUNG WOMAN: I don't want you to reject me again.

OLDER WOMAN: Come then!

YOUNG WOMAN: Promise!

OLDER WOMAN: But. . .

YOUNG WOMAN: But what?

OLDER WOMAN: No, nothing, but. . .

YOUNG WOMAN: But? . . .

OLDER WOMAN: Do you really want to? You really want to? Forget it, I didn't say anything. You're so young. And I. . .

YOUNG WOMAN: And you?

OLDER WOMAN: You know what I mean.

YOUNG WOMAN: You're only thirty-five.

OLDER WOMAN: No. Thirty-six.

YOUNG WOMAN: Yes. So?

OLDER WOMAN: I'm a lot older than you are.

YOUNG WOMAN: What you're saying is childish, stupid.

OLDER WOMAN: It's all of that. This new feeling. It's always that way.

YOUNG WOMAN: I don't understand. And I'm not as young as all that. You know that's true.

OLDER WOMAN: (*Ironic*) That's right. You've seen it all. Maybe, in fact, you're even older than I am?

YOUNG WOMAN: What?

OLDER WOMAN: Take it easy. You don't understand. I was joking. Just to laugh. (*Asks herself*) What time is it? . . . Time laughs at us, let's laugh a little as well, us too. . . But you didn't tell me. Where were you? And what's that we're hearing? Is that a noise? Don't you hear it?

YOUNG WOMAN: You tease! You heard exactly what I said, what I said before. OK, Darling, you win. I'm not coming anywhere near you.

OLDER WOMAN: Oh no! No. Were you running away from me? Were you running? Was that it? Come over here, please.

YOUNG WOMAN: No. I was behind the tree. I'll come in a minute. But wait! OK? On one condition! OK? OK? Close your eyes.

OLDER WOMAN: No. Not that. Not that. You know we can't do that. We can't close our eyes. I'm too afraid. Not that. OK? A noise! Do you hear it?

YOUNG WOMAN: Some people in the pass, on the path to the hill, below us, among the trees that are still standing, despite the catastrophe—a handful of trees, an army.

OLDER WOMAN: Maybe they're coming towards us?

YOUNG WOMAN: No. That's impossible. We're perched among the trees. We're well hidden behind this old one. It's impossible. No path leads to the tree where we are. Nobody sees us, but we see everything. Come on! We can't hear them anymore. Close your eyes. Don't cheat.

Long Pause.

OLDER WOMAN: I'm still hearing something. There's something. Is it you? Huh? Huh?

Beat.

Where are you? What are you doing? What have you been doing all this time? Tell me!

Beat.

> Say something. Say something. I'm afraid. Just a word. I'm afraid. Say something.

Beat.

> Where are you? Is that you?

YOUNG WOMAN: Shussh! Shussh! Listen to the silence. The anguish. The fear—fear that it's coming back to devastate us again.

OLDER WOMAN: Devastate?

YOUNG WOMAN: Devastate, yes. Devastate. Listen to the silence it makes.

OLDER WOMAN: No. I don't want to listen to that. Say something. Say something. I don't want silence. Say something! I want the sound of your voice. To know you're there. That a soul. . . I want to know, to hear life next to me. That I hear. . . No, no more silence or anguish around me. Please. Where are you? Tell me. Tell me. Where are you? Answer me! Answer me! Answer me, please!

Beat.

YOUNG WOMAN: (*She comes back*) I'm here.

OLDER WOMAN: You scared me. I was afraid. Don't ever do that again.

YOUNG WOMAN: (*She slips on a military uniform with the insignia of the United States on the sleeve. The jacket is wide open, revealing her breasts.*) Look at me now. I put on my equipment. We're going to dance. Dance with me.

OLDER WOMAN: What? Your equipment? What are you talking about? But. . .what. . .what is it?

YOUNG WOMAN: (*She has a boom box in her hand. We hear a few bars of Mambo music wafting from it.*) Yes, look at me! Want to dance?

OLDER WOMAN: Oh! Where'd you get that?

YOUNG WOMAN: From him. Before he left the earth. Isn't it something? I have one for you too.

OLDER WOMAN: You do?

YOUNG WOMAN: Do you want it? Do you want it now?

OLDER WOMAN: Another uniform? How did you do it?

YOUNG WOMAN: I saw him pass. Yes. He was on top of me. During the catastrophe; it was his back that protected me. Come on! Come and dance. Come next to me. It's over now. Take this, take your equipment. Get dressed. We're going to dance.

OLDER WOMAN: And then what. . .

YOUNG WOMAN: You really want to know? Do you?

OLDER WOMAN: You said, you saw him pass?

YOUNG WOMAN: (*Ironic*) No.

OLDER WOMAN: That's what I heard.

YOUNG WOMAN: No. He didn't just pass.

OLDER WOMAN: Well, what then?

YOUNG WOMAN: I mean: he was still breathing. I could've pulled him out of it. He was wounded, but he could have lived some more, again. I could have helped him. But. . .

OLDER WOMAN: But?

Pause.

YOUNG WOMAN: I didn't want him to live. I didn't want him to go on living. I helped him. It's me. I helped him die.

OLDER WOMAN: Are you sure? Are you really sure of that?

YOUNG WOMAN: I don't know. But in the end, he's not here, is he?

OLDER WOMAN: You're right. You're right. Let's forget it. You're right. Relief. After the catastrophe, some relief. At least that.

YOUNG WOMAN: Yes. And so I took this thing, his radio, and then the uniform. I thought it could somehow be useful, that I could make something of it. You never know. It was such a symbol for him. With it on, he looked like a hero. All those international military uniforms. So what about a heroine? A woman soldier? Now I'm a soldier, a heroine, as well.

OLDER WOMAN: Come to me, my heroine. Come offer me that dance. Come shake your ass in my face. We have to celebrate what you've done. Come on. Let's dance. Let's dance. Until we're drunk.

They dance.

You shimmy. Your shimmy's so fine I could die from it. You shimmy like a snake. You shimmy and we fly away!

YOUNG WOMAN: Hey! Take off your dress! Take it off! Slip this on. You, too. Here!

OLDER WOMAN: Really?

YOUNG WOMAN: Go ahead. A game. It's just a game. Don't you want it?

OLDER WOMAN: Yeah, I want your toy.

YOUNG WOMAN: Yes, right? Yes. Huh?

OLDER WOMAN: Why? Huh?

YOUNG WOMAN: Huh?

OLDER WOMAN: Huh? Huh?

YOUNG WOMAN: To exorcize the Evil, all the Evil that's surrounding us.

OLDER WOMAN: To exorcize it? You think so? To exorcize it? Yeah?

YOUNG WOMAN: Go ahead! Do it!

OLDER WOMAN: Wait! Wait!

YOUNG WOMAN: Take it, Baby!

OLDER WOMAN: Give it here. (*She slips on the military uniform with the insignia of the United Nations/France on the sleeve.*) We're well armed now! So now we can dance. Let's!

They dance again.

YOUNG WOMAN: (*She moves away abruptly*) Wait a minute. Wait.

OLDER WOMAN: (*She pulls The Young One brutally towards her.*) Where are you going?

From here on the theatre is transformed into a tragic, surreal ritual. The Young One frees herself, runs behind the tree. She comes back wearing a strap-on dildo. She rushes The Oldest, forces the long tip of the dildo in her mouth, and The Oldest sucks it. Then she forces her down on all fours and savagely plays at sodomizing her. When she's done, The Young One stands up without emotion, hands the strap-on to The Oldest, who repeats with The Young One what has just happened to her. They play this game over and over. Meanwhile, a neon sign attached to one of the branches of the tree by an old frayed rope slowly lights up. It proclaims: OMNIA MORS AEQUAT (death makes everyone equal). We hear intoned the far-off voices of women.

The Song:

First there was a cracking. Then everything started to shake, to fall and fall, never stop falling. A cracking. Only a cracking. And man loses his footing. Stumbles. Falls. Collapses. Falls. Everything becomes dust. A veil of traveling dust. Even without wind, it travels. And the cry. From the people. The cry. The cry. And the agony of the children. The cry. The tall cry of the people. Tall towards the sky—an afternoon blue. Unaware. Blue. Like the cry of disenchantment itself. The cry. The surf. The cry of the sea in the distance. Its enchantment. Despite everything. The sea that sings, spirals. The sea. Its cry. The cry that humans don't hear, don't hear any more. Caught up in their own pain, their own cry, their sad cry that kills. That kills everything. Man, responsible for making the earth stagger, staggers in his turn. His whole face. White. White. Fine dust. Earth. Sweat. Blood. The human city is a veil. Its castles are stone. Reinforced concrete. The bride was beautiful. A funeral shroud. Who will marry this veiled city now? Who will marry this lost city? No one. No one to marry her. She'll stay where she is, the city. Nothing left of her body. Nothing standing up. Except the trees. And. . .And. . . at her feet, the sea. The cracking of the sea. The surf. The forgotten, soft surf. Oh! A cracking. A cracking in the baptismal founts. A cracking. That's what was first. Then our feet became unsteady. Our feet that stumbled, that never stumble, never. Our stumbling feet. That event that we'll never, ever, ever, forget—ever. That event of a few seconds that will take years and years to erase. Even centuries. It will take longer than a person's life. A cracking comes along. Like this song at its beginnings. Yes, a cracking. A cracking that will bring on another, and another, in infinite repetition. But even well before the big cracking, there was the leaving—of parrots, lizards, woodpeckers, hummingbirds, red-throated hummers, geckos, toads—all the animals. And more, more, more. The sea's snoring. The waves, the surf quieting down. The air as well. That cracking of just a few seconds. Infinitesimal time and a whole life. All those lives. Infinite sadness. But maybe at the end—hope. Hope again. Belief. Yes. The dream of the sleeping child. In this Calvary, this black hole, at the end of this cataclysm, this apocalypse—unrivaled hope. Perhaps, yes perhaps a new departure. Perhaps? Yes. A child waking up. Its becoming forever rewarded.

After this song, we hear the Mambo again.

End.

Translation of the Creole:

1. No one can sleep! No one, no one can sleep, with their heart at rest, in repose! Even if they wanted to, nobody! Nobody dares sleep any more! The appointment has been made. An appointment without a definite time. Because it can show up, come when it wants to, without warning. Nobody can sleep. Who wants to slip away like a star in the sky, die horribly?

2. Keep watch! Yes, keep watch! Take your place! Keep watch, all of us! Our eyes alert!

3. What, who can close their eyes to sleep?

4. Hey, look! A star!

5. We've been here keeping watch for days. Every day, us two, exposed, shaken, not sure why! I would have liked to lay my head down to sleep! I would have liked to lay my head down, but I'm staying here, at my place, keeping watch. I would have liked to relax a little. Me too, sleep a little, finally. Oh! Relax! Stretch out and sleep! But I can't manage to sleep. I can't manage. I can't. Even as weak as I am, nothing, I can't.

6. Shoot, star, slip away!

7. Counting stars. Why? Why do we need to count? Stars fall. Why should we count them? Why go crazy counting? What's the reason? Why are we doing this?

8. You're not answering? What are we doing? What is this?

9. What are we doing?

10. Another one! Hey, look, look!

11. How sad that is, isn't it! How sad that is, isn't it!

12. Such shame!

13. Such Sadness! Sadness!

14. All of that!

15. Oh, how could I have thought that? Oh! How did I dare say it?

16. What?

17. You don't understand?

18. And us? What do we do now?

19. Shut up! Shut up!

20. A beautiful shooting star to reconcile the spirit with itself! Another one!

21. Oh, let me touch you. I want to touch your body. Can I please just touch your body, a little? Only touch you?

N.B. *Bèl amou* (Beautiful Love) is the name of the pimp and the brothel to which these women have been attached. The place has fallen (*tonbe*). The man is dead (*tonbe*) a well.

POSTFACE

Writing the disaster during the disaster is impossible for me. Attempting to do so would empty out any capacity for reflection, for distance.

I'm not one of those dealers in words, those carrion poets of the dead, sniffing out catastrophes. *Lord save me from that!* And let's leave that specialization to story-telling sensationalists.

It's always been impossible for me to write about any kind of actual drama. All the same, when disaster is transformed into total collapse, when disaster turns into what was clearly foreseeable, when it whisks away hundreds of thousands of human lives, words suddenly become crazy. If those who normally take up words as they would take up arms don't seize their words in time, they risk being lost under a wash of senile discourse.

So what matters now is for those who know how to NAME to NAME. That way we might come to understand something, little by little.

Who doesn't know that Haiti, just like other countries dwelling sadly under the yoke of countless criminals, omniscient and omnipotent heads of State, was running (is still running) towards disaster? That's why, reflecting on the Great Drama of last January, we must quickly "relativize" it—in order to get to the truth.

The remorse raging in us—and there is a great deal of remorse—comes in recognizing that we could have avoided so many victims, so very many, if those responsible for running things had only made known to the population the risks of what was coming and how to take care of themselves.

The goal of this play is not, then, to illustrate the chronicle of a recent drama, but to illuminate a disaster already foretold, one that had been in the works far too long. No. This project means in no way to tell the story of a planetary event that had been announced for a very long time.

What has nourished my work from the first is speaking about a country that has stingily mired itself in such conspicuous Calamity, even if conscious of what was happening. In what I write, mother, father, son, and daughter hurl themselves at each other endlessly. And I keep seeing the family as if it were the key to the enigma. This time, of course, the context is even more tortuous for my two characters: the young one and the oldest...

Called by names that are almost familial, but also undefined: the young one, the oldest... My choice to create female figures who symbolize the great Haitian family—without given names that have been recognized by a government official or inscribed in court documents.

I especially wanted to construct a generational divide, in order to better illustrate the paradox of modern politics in this country (and in many others) in which those younger than 18 (more than half the country) don't participate in its political life. Because according to the "sacrosanct" laws of democracy—laws that pertain everywhere—the under 18s aren't allowed to vote. Others decide for them.

And a thundering silence...

In this play, far from themes I've already examined, such as migration, I wanted to treat through these two women a kind of self-decreed ostracism, an inability to speak that exists in every society ruled by decadent, phallocratic principles. I had no choice but to think about this after the earthquake—with so many victims (officially 316,000). The future of orphans, of widows...

And more generally, about the future of the oppressed, once the oppressor has disappeared and left a hole to fill. The double task of the woman (or the man) who must, from that point on, take their life in their own hands after years of abuse. Take charge of a life whose taste had been unavailable.

We can see the same thing in the formerly colonized, once the colonizer has left. And don't we, in fact, see elements of this in migration, in the act of return? Every colonized person tends to return to their colonizer. To keep a certain heritage alive, what Edouard Glissant terms "relation" (in his 2009 *La Philosophie de la relation*). There are many reasons for this: language, cultural affinities. . . All that to say that even when freed, there's a period of emptiness, of gap, a long period of searching before the formerly colonized re-appropriates their own history, takes firm control of their own lives.

This is unfortunately the case of many human beings, who, even liberated, have a very long path in front of them.

I chose, then, the context of the earthquake, this macabre event, as the launching place for Liberation, for Hope, for another possible Future. Instead of believing in a curse, I'm forcing myself to try to see the Earthquake as a happy metaphor, synonymous in every positive way with shake-up, reversal, and radical change. Because in the end what counts is not that the catastrophe happened (it's over), but that it can lead to a better future.

They won't stop calling what's happened "Apocalyptic," "Catastrophic," "Unfortunate." There aren't, in fact, the words for all those lost souls. And my heroines? No. They won't speak them. They have to get up, energetically take their stand. Like so many others born into tattered families, stuck in insoluble situations way before the earthquake—way before, since the glorious birth of a country that's been led by a pack of clowns. Like those others, these two women, faced with the executioner, faced with the entire world, they'll revolt, insisting that life is hard, yes, sometimes calamitous, very often unbelievable. But there's nothing more marvelous, more surprising.

And the Whole World Quakes (The Great Collapse): an experiment, an attempt at a wake-up call, a passage between silence and crying out, from muteness to speech. Nothing to tell. Just an effort to get words out. Gesticulations.

Two women perched on top of a hill after a great catastrophe, who count, taking stock. . .

> One. Two.
> Ten. One thousand.
> Two-hundred thousand.
> Keeping track.
> Counting those who counted for us.

Counting. Watching over. Yes, mourning. Leaving everything suspended in silence. Their first refuge. A groaning silence. Acrid. Inhabited. Uninhabited. The great collapse.

To reveal their fear. Their great disdain for evil. For masculinity. For everything wrong. The effort to believe in living again. To exist after that nameless thing. The ritual of continuing.

So here it is: two women. In that situation, in that becoming, such as it is. Themselves. And like them, others. In other times. On other destroyed lands. After a great war. A terrifying epidemic. After the terrible passage of evil.

Vile spectators. These two women are in front of us. They can't stop talking. They can't stop keeping silent. They'll never say everything. Just as we never manage to say everything in the theatre.

I admit that I submit to writing the way one gives oneself to a drug. It's at the end of the experience that I know what I've lived—what I've allowed myself to live. Each time, the same drive towards intoxication. Each time, the same pleasure of having been carried away.

I propose the same voyage to those who choose to come with me! A theatre trip as a dream of mankind. Theatre—my dream of the human.

FAMILY
by
Gaël Octavia

MARTINIQUE

translation by Katharine Woff & Lucie Tiberghien

CHARACTERS

THE MOTHER
THE FATHER
THE TEACHER
THE BOY
THE GIRL
NARRATOR (may be off stage)
CHILD'S VOICE (off stage)

THE MOTHER, THE FATHER, THE TEACHER, THE BOY *and* THE GIRL *may be played by two actors: a man and a woman.*

I – MOTHER

A dining room. A table, chairs. On the table: a knife and a nearly empty wine glass.

The mother is alone. She wears an apron. She has a bucket of water in one hand, a brush and a bottle of cleaning fluid in the other.

THE MOTHER: He'll come home. And he'll ask: where are the children?

The mother kneels down and scours the floor. We hear the sound of a key in the lock. The mother gets up hurriedly, puts away the bucket of water, the cleaning fluid and the scouring brush, takes off her apron, straightens herself out and fixes her hair.

The father enters.

The mother approaches him. He kisses her soberly on the cheek. She helps him take off his jacket.

THE FATHER: Where are the children?

THE MOTHER: They're in bed.

THE FATHER: Already?

THE MOTHER: It's bedtime. You're home late.

The father and mother sit at the table, facing each other.

THE MOTHER: So here we are. He's home, finally. . . he asked to see the children so I replied that it was late, that they were sleeping, and that he should absolutely not wake them. Next, I tried to talk about myself. (*To the father.*) I didn't make anything for dinner, my love. I didn't have time. I had a ton of things to do.

She looks at him.

He doesn't look at her.

THE MOTHER: Do you want wine?

The mother goes to find a bottle of wine.

The father picks up the wine glass on the table, examines it, smells it.

THE MOTHER *comes back with the bottle, opens it.*

THE MOTHER: It's clean. Would you prefer another glass?

The father shakes his head.

The mother serves him, sits down and looks at him, mute.

The father swirls the wine in the glass but doesn't drink it.

THE MOTHER: You're home late. I didn't cook. I didn't think you'd be coming home.

The father sets down the glass.

THE FATHER: Have the children been in bed for long?

THE MOTHER: And now he asks about the children again. (*She looks at her watch.*) No, not very long.

The father gets up.

THE FATHER: I'm going to tuck them in. Maybe they're not asleep.

THE MOTHER: No!

THE FATHER: I have to tuck my little girl in. I didn't tuck her in last night.

THE MOTHER: It's too late.

THE FATHER: Are you sure?

THE MOTHER: Yes.

The father sits back down.

The mother goes up to him. She massages his shoulders and neck firmly, vigorously. There is no sensuality in this gesture. It's more like that of a sports coach.

We see from the father's expression that it's hurting him.

THE FATHER: Ouch!

THE MOTHER: (*Stopping*) What?

THE FATHER: Nothing. It feels good.

The mother goes back to massaging. She becomes more and more tender.

THE MOTHER: I'm a massage expert. But I don't want to be a professional. I only massage my husband.

She kisses him.

THE FATHER: The children. . .

THE MOTHER: They're in bed!

She tries to kiss him again but knocks over the glass of wine that spills onto the table.

THE FATHER: They're going to hear us. The children. . .

THE MOTHER: They're sleeping like logs. They won't hear anything. We have the house to ourselves.

THE FATHER: You spilled wine on my tie.

The mother stops. She moves away from the father. She refills the glass.

THE MOTHER: Are you hungry? Did you eat out?

THE FATHER: No.

THE MOTHER: There's ham.

She goes out and comes back with a large plate of ham.

The father is pensive.

She looks at him, plate in hand.

THE MOTHER: He's thinking about the children.

She places the plate of ham on the table.

The father does not eat.

THE FATHER: There's no school tomorrow. Let's do something special for the little one's birthday.

THE MOTHER: Her birthday is on Sunday.

THE FATHER: I know.

THE MOTHER: Of course he knows.

THE FATHER: We can do something special on Sunday too. But I cancelled all my meetings for tomorrow. I'm taking a day off.

THE MOTHER: I can't tomorrow. I have to do the laundry.

THE FATHER: We could take them to the countryside. Go horseback-riding. And canoeing.

THE MOTHER: I can't.

THE FATHER: No problem. I can take them by myself.

THE MOTHER: Thanks for understanding.

THE FATHER: We'll pack a picnic.

THE MOTHER: Thanks for understanding. He's not "understanding." He's thrilled. He says "We're going to do something special." "We," that's him and the children.

THE FATHER: Hard-boiled eggs, bananas, chocolate, bread, ham.

THE MOTHER: Do you want some ham, darling?

THE FATHER: We'll go to the river. We haven't been to the river since the children. They'd like it, the river, don't you think? They say the little white shed where we rented our canoes back then is closed. Do you think there's another rental place? Do you think it's still possible to go canoeing in the river?

THE MOTHER: Yes, it is. (*Pause*) He's still thinking about the children. It was my son's birthday three months ago. My husband hadn't come home all week. The birthday was on Friday. My husband wasn't there. I didn't know where he was. I made a cake, I put on some music, the children wore Mickey Mouse ears and we had a party. A sad little party for the three of us. On Saturday morning my husband tiptoed in. And on Saturday afternoon he took my son to a soccer game. The sad little party was forgotten. My son said, "Daddy, I am so happy. So happy to be with you!" When I tucked him in, that Saturday night, he said the same to me, "Mommy, I was so happy. So happy to be at the game with Daddy!" It was the most wonderful day of his life.

THE FATHER: It must be possible to rent canoes somewhere. Kayaks.

THE MOTHER: Do you remember the first time we went canoeing? Maybe you've forgotten. My father had organized a celebration for my high school graduation. A gorgeous old house in the countryside, rented for a few days. All my friends. And my friends' friends. There was a river and canoes. We raced. Bertrand was there. Handsome, big and strong Bertrand. There were other young men my age, with biceps like that. Handsome. And then you, a bit skinny but also handsome. We organized a race, and I was on a team with Bertrand who was in love with me of course, and who was in fact my boyfriend. And I won because Bertrand was the strongest. I was such a flirt back then; I said that after the picnic, I'd team up with someone else. And after the picnic I teamed up with you; the skinniest one. And I still won. We were the quickest, despite our skinny arms. And you said it was because we were in perfect harmony. Because we were telepathically connected. I didn't think I was reading your mind at all. But you said that, telepathy, even though you didn't have to.

THE FATHER: At the very least, let's go to Aqualand!

THE MOTHER: The little one's teacher wants to see you.

THE FATHER: Excuse me?

THE MOTHER: You're called in. I don't know what she did.

THE FATHER: My little girl?

THE MOTHER: She came home last night and said: "The teacher wants to see Daddy because of me." She said that, while handing me her notebook; "The teacher wants to see Daddy."

THE FATHER: When?

THE MOTHER: Next Tuesday at 6.

THE FATHER: I'll go.

THE MOTHER: He'll go. He'll go. Her notebook mentions that her parents are called in next Tuesday at 6. I think the teacher said: "I want to see your parents" and the little one extrapolated. Or maybe the teacher even said: "I want to see your mother" because I'm the one who goes to PTA meetings. But I think the little one wanted her teacher to finally meet her father. Because she loves her teacher, who is of course young, skinny, beautiful and single, and because she loves her father. I have no idea what she did that led to this. But I think her father and her teacher meeting was the goal.

THE FATHER: Next Tuesday at 6.

THE MOTHER: That's it. The goal. You're not drinking your wine, darling?

She drinks from his glass and starts to laugh loudly as if she were already drunk.

THE FATHER: Stop, you're going to wake the children!

THE MOTHER: He's still talking about the children. Why does it surprise me every time? I believe he's listening to me. That he feels me, that he empathizes with me. I laugh and I think he'll laugh with me. I shiver and I hope he'll snuggle up to me. I drink red wine and I imagine we'll get drunk together. Ever since that first canoeing trip, I believed it was true, that we were "telepathically connected." I felt like I could always read his thoughts and I was certain he read mine like a book. Back then, he never misunderstood me, and as far as I can tell, he didn't cheat on me either.

She takes another sip of wine and staggers a bit.

THE FATHER: Careful, don't spill.

THE MOTHER: Oh, I'm allowed to relax a little! I had a hard day, you know. Don't you want to know what I did today, my love?

THE FATHER: What did you do today?

THE MOTHER: Guess.

THE FATHER: Today's Tuesday. You went to the supermarket.

THE MOTHER: Well done! You guessed correctly! On Tuesdays, I go to the supermarket. On Wednesdays, I do the laundry. I am a very well structured housewife. The children were ill this morning. They didn't go to school.

THE FATHER: They're ill?

THE MOTHER: No, they were faking. It was too late by the time I realized. They missed school.

THE FATHER: You should have taken them anyway! They'll do it again otherwise.

THE MOTHER: The school doesn't accept students more than two hours late, my love.

THE FATHER: And this afternoon? They missed this afternoon too? Why didn't you take them this afternoon?

THE MOTHER: I'd have liked to see you try! They were impossible today. The boy didn't want to eat his lunch. He tipped over his plate onto the table, the little pig, and his sister copied him. I had to wrestle with them, you know. They don't respect anything, the little bastards. Nothing will stop them. They've decided to drive me crazy. They stopped when I said they could come with me to the supermarket. They need. . . you should. . . they need you to punish them sometimes. But you'd have to be here for that. You. . .

THE FATHER: And it went okay, at the supermarket?

THE MOTHER: They had finally calmed down. Not me, however. I was so annoyed. Completely overwhelmed. The place was packed with people. I don't get it. Even during the week now, all these people shopping, filling up their carts, stripping the shelves. We were like an army of ants running through the aisles. There were deals everywhere! I don't understand that either. Everything's a deal. Everything's a special offer. Deals on vegetables. Deals on detergents. There was even a deal on this miracle product that cleans everything! This detergent I absolutely need. . .

THE FATHER: Good, it turned out well in the end. But I don't want them to miss school anymore.

The father stands.

THE MOTHER: What are you doing?

THE FATHER: I'm going.

THE MOTHER: You're not interested.

THE FATHER: No, no, I am. But I have to go to work.

THE MOTHER: At this hour?

THE FATHER: I'm my own boss. I don't have a schedule.

THE MOTHER: You're not going to work.

THE FATHER: I have to go.

THE MOTHER: Why are you talking about work? Why are you talking without looking at me? I bore you. (*Pause*) I can see that I bore you. I understand why. The children's lunch. The price of detergent. But I used to shine, before. I was a well brought-up young woman. I was very intelligent, you know. My teachers were thrilled. They said so, to my father. Your daughter is a pearl. Your daughter is a diamond. I used to shine just like a diamond. I was the pride of my father and the great love of my big brother. Do you know that all my brother's girlfriends used to be jealous. They would stand there simpering. But what choice did they have, faced with a diamond? And then something happened. I met you and instead of shining, I began to burn. I went from diamond to charcoal. I consumed all my energy making your life better, easier. And life smiled on you. The more energy I consumed, the more successful you became. But I was happy. I was proud. I thought that that was what being your wife was. I thought I was exemplary. Now you look at me like I'm a pile of ashes, but it's for you that I burned.

THE FATHER: Thank you.

THE MOTHER: My burning brought you all your victories. And each victory brought you more. . . admirers. How ironic. Today this pile of ashes bores you and you spend your nights elsewhere.

THE FATHER: I'm working.

THE MOTHER: If only you admitted it. If you told me to my face: "Darling, you bore me." If you told me what to do, I would do it, you know. And if you admitted that there's nothing I can do, I would accept my lot. I would disappear. Instead you say nothing. You give me nothing. You pretend it's your work or the children. But it would be better, you know, if you spoke less about the children and instead were there in the morning when they wake up. Maybe they would be less difficult. Oh I know, they don't give you a hard time about anything. They forgive you for everything. You leave for a week and when you tiptoe back in, one morning, you get "Daddy, I'm so happy!"

THE FATHER: Are you done?

THE MOTHER: Done? I'll never be done! You can screw whoever you want but this will never be done.

THE FATHER: I'm going to tuck in the children.

THE MOTHER: The children, always the children! What am I supposed to say? That I cut the children's throats? The children aren't here, my love, they're at Mamie's.

THE FATHER: Why are they at Mamie's? What's wrong?

THE MOTHER: Well, they need to see their grandmother, don't they? Mamie complains that they're growing up too fast. I wanted us to have the evening to ourselves. And it was the right thing to do, since you came back.

He sighs and sits back down.

She stands behind him and timidly caresses his shoulders.

THE MOTHER: Please. You can't say no every time. Relax.

She strokes his face. She gives him the glass of wine.

He drinks.

She picks up pieces of ham and feeds him.

He chews slowly.

THE MOTHER: See? See how you're able to relax? You're showing me your real face and I recognize you. See: nothing is done.

She tries to put another piece in his mouth.

He sighs.

THE MOTHER: No. . . I was dreaming, right? Your face is closing up. Your night face. . .

She starts to cry. She pulls away from him slowly, sits on her chair.

She sobs, head in hands.

THE FATHER: Don't cry, please.

THE MOTHER: I don't want to cry. . . but. . . you're not. . . relaxed.

THE FATHER: I. . . the children. I don't like when you drop them off like that, without warning me. You know they don't like going to Mamie's. They get bored at Mamie's. Here they have their toys, their universe, their bedroom. They find the bedrooms at Mamie's gloomy.

THE MOTHER: At Mamie's they each have their own bedroom.

THE FATHER: Exactly. You know they don't like that. Our girl is going to have nightmares without her brother nearby.

THE MOTHER: Stop pitying them! You don't know them. Not any more than you know me. You don't know this house, this house that you leave and return to in silence. You don't belong to this house and you're wrong about everything. You're wrong about them.

THE FATHER: Stop. Leave the children out of this.

THE MOTHER: Out of this? But how is that possible: they're completely in it. They were born in it. They belong to this story. Out of this... (*She laughs.*) First, you should know that your children are little pigs. Little bastards. They torture me. They defy my authority. And you, they idolize. They respect you despite your infidelities. They have no morals. They're completely perverted. They sleep in the same room, in the same bed. They do things, you know. They're too old to share a bed. I've said it a hundred times but who listens to me? They act like little pigs. They deserve to have their throats slit like pigs and be turned into ham!

She approaches his mouth with a piece of ham.

The father stops chewing suddenly and pushes her hand away.

THE FATHER: Where are the children?

THE MOTHER: Eat!

The father pushes away the plate.

The mother gets up, finds her bucket and brush and returns to scrubbing the floor.

THE FATHER: What are you doing?

THE MOTHER: I'm working.

The father rises.

THE FATHER: What's all this blood?

He walks up to her.

The mother doesn't respond and continues to scrub.

THE FATHER: What's all this blood? Answer me! (*She doesn't respond. He grabs hold of her shoulders.*) Answer me!

THE MOTHER: (*Still scrubbing*) It's my blood...

The father lets her go. He looks at her for a moment, unsure.

She scrubs harder.

THE MOTHER: It's my blood and yours. Our blood flowing together, joined in a holy matrimonial layer. This is our blood, intertwined, indistinguishable. Proof of our oath. Proof of love. Proof of what you said, long ago, in that canoe, with the waves below as a witness. We were in perfect harmony. We had a telepathic connection. We understood each other. Brother and sister. One single soul. You didn't have to say that.

THE FATHER: (*Looking at her blood-streaked hands*) It can't be.

THE MOTHER: Without love, a woman becomes a witch. And witches don't respect laws. They invert the order of the world. There's only one way to cancel a promise. You have to go back in time. I wanted to have never heard your promise. I wanted to be a virgin again. Return to my father's side, my brother's side. Be the girl I used to be. Return to the blessed time of my childhood.

THE FATHER: Where are my children?

THE MOTHER: They're at Mamie's. They're fine.

THE FATHER: Tell me the truth. Where are my children?

THE MOTHER: Shhhh! They're ill. They're sleeping. Don't wake them.

THE FATHER: Where are my children, please! Please!

THE MOTHER: I don't know where your children are! I lost them at the supermarket. I was tired. I'd argued with my son. I'd carried my daughter on my back. I was worn out and there was this miracle detergent, this cheap cleaning product, really cheap, on the other side of the store. I left them near the chocolate, near the candy, or near the ice cream, I don't know any more. I said I'd be back right away. I said if they were good we'd buy some chocolate. Or ice cream. I left them for five minutes. They were wearing me out. Five minutes. When I came back they were gone.

THE FATHER: And where are they now?

THE MOTHER: I had the detergent in my hand. I needed the detergent for the blood. And the children: gone!

THE FATHER: My God, where are my children? Tell me, crazy woman!

THE MOTHER: You didn't have to say that. You didn't have to say it.

THE FATHER: What have you done?

The mother stands up suddenly.

THE MOTHER: Without a father, there is no mother. (*She gets back on her knees and begins to scrub.*) I have to clean. I have to clean up the blood. (*She scrubs harder. She also scrubs the walls.*) Children ruin everything. Without the blood of my children, this house would be white, monochrome and clean. And we would be so happy, my love.

THE FATHER: Be quiet! Be quiet!

THE MOTHER: They hated me so much this morning. They hated me for not knowing how to keep you home.

THE FATHER: Be quiet!

THE MOTHER: They kept asking where you were. They accused me. They threatened me.

THE FATHER: Forgive me. Forgive me, my children.

He curls up on the floor in the fetal position.

THE MOTHER: I carried them in my belly. And I carried you in my arms. And after all that, it's as if you expected me to leave you alone. But you would have held it against me, if I'd left. So I am here.

After a moment, the mother finally stops scrubbing.

THE MOTHER: My love! Is something wrong, my love? (*She approaches him.*) My love, my lover, my guiding star.

She wraps herself around his body. She rocks him.

They stay like this for a moment, him crying, her rocking him like a baby. We suddenly hear a child's voice.

THE CHILD: Daddy!

Blackout.

II – FATHER

NARRATOR: A journey home. This is the story of a man walking the streets of a city. A man dressed in a grey suit and tie, slightly scruffy. Maybe, this is a man returning home after a particularly difficult day at work. Most likely, it is a man with an unremarkable face but a quick stride. Feet that stop at the door of a building. A door that opens. A man that returns home.

On the stage, a table and chairs. On the table, a glass and an open bottle of wine.

The father, in a grey suit, enters. We hear the voice of a little girl coming from another room.

THE GIRL: Daddy!

The father turns his back to the audience. He stays like this for a few seconds, then turns around again, facing the audience.

THE FATHER: (*Speaking very sweetly*) A kiss. She wants a kiss.

THE GIRL: Daddy!

The father sighs and rubs his face. He looks up. He sighs again. Then, suddenly, he takes off his jacket, throws it on a chair, takes off his shirt and uses it to wipe his face and chest.

THE GIRL: Daddy!

The father exits. We hear the sound of water running, then the sound of someone brushing their teeth.

THE GIRL: Daddy!

The father returns to the stage, chest bare, a towel around his neck. He stops, facing the audience for a few moments. He hesitates and looks around. He sees the glass and the bottle of wine on the table. He goes to the table, sits, uncorks the wine and smells it. He closes his eyes. Then he stands, wipes his face and chest with the towel.

THE FATHER: Sweetheart?

The father leaves the stage. We hear him climbing stairs, then we hear a door open and close. A few seconds later, we hear him slowly come back downstairs. He reappears on stage.

THE FATHER: Too late. She fell asleep. (*He goes to the table and pours himself a glass of wine.*) A kiss. I guess all she wanted was I kiss. (*He drinks.*) I already missed her last night. I would have liked to have given her one tonight. A kiss. I don't know why I panic like that, every time.

He exits and re-enters with a big plate of ham. He sits at the table and eats.

THE FATHER: Pork and silence. It's incredible how depressing it is to eat cold meat alone. Especially given that they're all there, behind these walls. . . (*He interrupts himself to eat.*) It always reminds me of my childhood meals. Eight of us at the table around a steaming pot of soup, every evening. Father, mother and six children, under a light so glaring it pierced us through and through. We never would have had a meal without my father. We would have waited for him until the middle of the night if we had to. (*He interrupts himself to eat once more.*) To be honest, I prefer this to having to sit through her making a scene. I prefer knowing my wife has gone to bed at 8 to punish me, than hearing her tell me, looking like a madonna born without sin, that my little girl waited for her daddy all day. I prefer that my son closes his eyes in a hurry when I enter his room, than having to read in those same eyes, how much I've been gone. I prefer to eat in the dark, to be forgotten, to feel as if I've entered like a thief. But still, I would have liked to have given my little girl a kiss. Or at least, managed to explain to my wife why I didn't give my little girl a kiss. That's what it is: I would have liked to have had a chance to convince her that my reasons are solid. (*He interrupts himself to eat again. He eats greedily, chokes a bit and starts to cough.*) It's not because I have the flu that I didn't kiss my daughter tonight. And it's obviously not because of the countless viruses, bacteria, microbes, illnesses which flourish on public transportation. In the end, the reason why isn't very important. What's important is that I sincerely wanted to give her her daily ration of kisses and make up for yesterday's. My little girl would have told me about her day and asked about mine. And I would have told her about it, being careful of course, to leave one part out.

He goes back to eating.

NARRATOR: Paths crossing. This is the story of a man walking the streets of a city. His face has nothing noteworthy. He wears a suit that is elegant yet casual, grey. This is the story of another man who also blends into the crowd. No distinguishing features. He's elegant yet simple, dressed in black. This is about two men, cloaked in respectability, crossing paths on the street in a city. A grey suit and a black suit that meet each other, stop, cling on to each other. It is about two bodies that cross paths and a kiss. Two men that cross paths and hold each other.

THE FATHER: It's the smell! Not the flu, the smell. Something that would have been left behind against my will. Something I refuse to let into my home. Something tenacious like a smell or a look on my face. I can't give my little girl a kiss if I'm not certain of being rid of it.

He stops eating, clears the table, exits the stage, then returns empty-handed.

THE FATHER: I just want to return home looking like a father who has spent his day doing his fatherly duty.

He puts his shirt and jacket back on and sits in his chair. He seems to be waiting for someone.

The teacher, particularly pretty, enters the stage.

The father stands to shake her hand.

THE TEACHER: (*With a big smile*) Nice to meet you.

THE FATHER: And you as well.

She stares at him for a moment.

The father sits back down.

The teacher sits on the edge of the table. Her gestures are sensual.

THE FATHER: Well?

THE TEACHER: Oh, your daughter? She's adorable, really adorable. And... very smart. She's clearly ahead of the rest of the class in math, in reading... a really very smart little girl.

THE FATHER: But? You haven't called me in because she's the smartest in her class.

THE TEACHER: No, of course. Yet... Why only give bad news?

She laughs.

THE FATHER: So?

THE TEACHER: She's a little... provocative.

THE FATHER: Provocative?

THE TEACHER: Provocative. She kisses boys.

THE FATHER: She kisses boys? Is there a classmate she likes?

THE TEACHER: All the boys. She has kissed all the boys in the class. And also the boys in the other classes. And she's shown them her panties.

THE FATHER: Ah...

The father stands. He takes several steps before returning to face the teacher.

THE FATHER: And you find this worrisome?

THE TEACHER: Don't you?

THE FATHER: I don't know. It's not terrible. I'm sorry, it's just that I was quite worried, coming here. I must have imagined something really serious.

THE TEACHER: Really serious? Listen, I don't think we should downplay what your daughter has done.

THE FATHER: Oh, it's fine! She's eight years old! Can she really be a flirt at age eight? Don't you think it's just child's play? That she isn't aware of what she's doing?

THE TEACHER: All I'm doing is noting facts. Facts shouldn't be denied and reasons should be determined.

She looks at him intensely.

He walks away.

THE FATHER: Paths crossing. This is the story of a little girl in a playground, and it's this little girl's father who kisses a man on the street in a city. It's a playground's story that crosses paths with an adult story. (*He indicates the teacher.*) She knows. She presumes that if my little girl kisses boys it's because I myself kiss boys. She thinks my little girl is provocative and perverted because I am debauched and perverted. (*He returns to the teacher, sits on the edge of the table next to her.*) I assume that now is the time to ask myself if it's my fault.

THE TEACHER: I didn't insinuate anything of the sort.

THE FATHER: She knows. She's been watching my every move from the start, like a cop. She read it on my face. She smelled something. (*To the teacher*) But it must be a little bit my fault, no? Why else?

The teacher bursts out laughing.

THE TEACHER: You are interesting. (*She looks at him intensely for several seconds.*) You know, I really appreciate that you feel responsible. It's not that common, among fathers. Most defer responsibility onto the mother. Men are so selfish.

THE FATHER: Selfish. . .

THE TEACHER: But not you. (*Pause*) Whatever the reason for your daughter's behavior, I am here to help you. I'm completely at your disposal.

She takes his hand.

THE FATHER: You are very kind.

THE TEACHER: (*Keeping his hand between hers*) Your daughter is very precocious. Very mature and intuitive too. I had a little talk with her. She insinuated that you're having marital difficulties.

THE FATHER: (*Taking back his hand*) Excuse me (*He stands and turns his back to her.*) It's a test, the hand. She's testing me, clearly. A real cop. (*He returns to face the teacher.*) Let's stick to the point.

THE TEACHER: Do you find me attractive?

The father turns away from the teacher again.

THE FATHER: She knows! (*Facing the teacher again*) Very much. Like everyone, I imagine. But, as it turns out, I'm married. You must know that. It must be mentioned in my daughter's file. Married, not divorced, not separated, not a single father.

The teacher laughs.

THE TEACHER: You don't need to keep repeating it. I did read the file and. . . I don't care that you're married.

THE FATHER: Ah. . . you're. . . tricky. (*He walks away from the teacher.*) Now I'm completely confused. (*To the teacher*) I mean. . . don't women feel any solidarity towards other women? My wife loves me, you know. (*He turns away again and moves even further from her.*) My wife loves me. The less she understands me the more she loves me. As if that was precisely what love is: being attracted to not understanding and letting yourself become fascinated by what you don't understand. The more time passes, the more curious my wife is about me. I am a case study. She wants to get inside my head, settle in there so she can nose about and flush me out. This endless quest connects us for the rest of our lives. On my end, I try to treat her well. But I think that where love is concerned, half measures aren't worth anything. She suffers. She's decided I have mistresses and I let her believe it. She's consumed by her despair, it breaks her bones, but to me that seems more acceptable than the truth. She keeps hoping she'll regain control. Be the most beautiful again, which she is, in fact. (*He turns back to the teacher.*) I forgot to tell you: my wife is very beautiful. Even more beautiful than you.

THE TEACHER: Beautiful but unremarkable. Common.

THE FATHER: She's confident. I don't know how I'm going to get out of this.

THE TEACHER: You know, I've met her many times, your wife. It's true, she's beautiful. But so sad! Dissatisfied. Alone. You take one look at her and you immediately know that her husband is that type.

The father returns to sit on the table.

THE FATHER: That type of man?

THE TEACHER: She should take a lover, your wife. She's really quite pretty, after all. Men must like her.

THE FATHER: I wish her that and more. That type of man, you said. What type of man?

THE TEACHER: You know full well what I'm talking about.

He looks at her interrogatively.

THE TEACHER: Oh, stop playing! Just kiss me.

He hesitates, then kisses her for a long time. And then he stops suddenly.

THE FATHER: On that note, goodbye.

He gets up.

THE TEACHER: No. You don't want to leave, and neither do I.

The father takes two or three steps downstage, then stops.

THE TEACHER: You are that type of man. I knew it. Your desire to frustrate me is just as strong as your desire alone. You're really twisted. Come back!

THE FATHER: You understand everything, don't you.

THE TEACHER: I've known a few men like you. I'm not surprised your kid is so disturbed.

THE FATHER: Stop!

THE TEACHER: Come back and face it! Come back, you dirty selfish shit!

The father advances all the way to the front of the stage.

The light on the teacher dims throughout.

THE TEACHER: By the way, she also kissed her brother, your kid.

The teacher is totally in the dark. She disappears completely.

THE TEACHER: Come back! You're really the king of bastards.

The father, now alone on stage, stands still downstage.

THE FATHER: Can you believe this?

The light returns progressively upstage. The teacher has exited.

The father crosses upstage to make sure she's no longer there.

THE FATHER: I don't know why I've always had complicated relationships with women. It started with my mother. She had six sons so she had her pick. But she had to focus on me. Me, who was neither the oldest nor the youngest. Me, the fourth one. . . I never understood. And then came my wife. (*Pause*) I loved my wife. I think. Or maybe I thought I loved women and she was just the nicest. We got married. We had the children. We had a son, first. I figured it out. . . all this, men. . . I figured it out on the evening of my son's birth. I was done with work. I was running to the maternity ward. I was going to be a dad. And that's when the story happened. Paths crossed. A kiss was exchanged between two men in a street. An accident. A catastrophic incident that took me far away from my wife and children. I saw my son being born while my head was elsewhere, my senses monopolized by a man, my body gnawed away by desire for a man. They put my son in my arms. My son, the one I dreamed of, the one I waited for. . . and all I wanted was to place him there, on his mother's breast, in order to go find my lover. My son. . . the truth is, I don't even remember him coming into this world. I didn't see his little head coming out, his little red body, so little but so prodigiously alive. I had a different body in my head. I don't remember his first cry. My memory is saturated by other cries, gasps, breaths. My memory holds onto these clandestine cries and allows them to take over, because outside my head, these cries don't officially exist. I saw him again, this guy, the very next day. And I punched his face in, because he had stolen my son's birth from me.

He exits the stage and comes back with a little tape recorder.

THE FATHER: Of course, there were other instances of paths crossing. Always by accident. Always while I was desperately trying to return home. I record the children now. Sometimes without their knowing. I record their voices because I am more sensitive to sound than images and because my mind punishes me by erasing the memory of my children's voice. My children's words. My children's laughter. Privileges of good fathers.

He turns on the tape recorder. We hear the laugh of children. The father looks lovingly at the tape recorder and laughs. In the middle of the laughs we hear a woman's voice.

THE MOTHER's voice: You're making a mess, darlings.

The father turns off the tape recorder.

THE FATHER: My wife. . . (*Pause*) I would have liked be friends with her. I should have left her as soon as I realized, as soon as crossed paths with that first man. (*Pause*) On the day of my son's birth. But would that have been worse, in the end? I don't know if my wife would have wanted to become my best friend. I also don't know if she would have taken my son away from me. I suppose that at the time, I imagined the worst. (*Pause*) I tried to return to her, to return to our life. I believe I was happy before that first man. I've completely forgotten that time, even though my wife brings it up constantly, but I'm certain it was a happy time. One year after everything fell apart, a little while before the birth of my daughter, I took a break. Like a smoker, but without a substitute to chew on or patch on my body. I left a man whom I loved, out of love for my unborn daughter. I didn't want to miss my daughter, her little bald head and her animal cry.

He turns the tape recorder back on. We hear a baby cry.

THE FATHER: I was awful, just like a smoker in the midst of trying to quit. After weeks of abstinence, I was even more obsessed with forbidden bodies, clandestine breaths. (*He sighs. Pause.*) I remember my daughter's birth even less than my son's. As they were taking her out of her mother's belly, all I could see was the face of the first man I loved. I was hearing my lover's sobs, and my own, mixed together. The sobs of the day I left him. I was further than ever from the hospital room, totally outside my body. I didn't take my daughter in my arms when the nurse handed her to me, for fear of hurting her, for fear of dropping her or biting her. I was at once an exhausted specter and an uncontrollable Minotaur. As early as the next day, I went to town in search of that man, my first true love. I didn't find him, but as before life began again.

He presses Play again on the tape recorder. We hear the voice of a little boy.

THE BOY: Daddy, I'm so happy! So happy!

THE FATHER: My children are not unhappy. We always manage to reconnect, no matter how long or how intense my absences are. They think I go on trips. I too feel like I'm on a trip. I often think of that other traveller who spent so many years to find Ithaca. He didn't choose his wandering any more than I chose mine, but, upon his return, no-one recognized him, not even his son. My son closed his eyes tonight when I entered his room. Will there be a day when my son no longer recognizes me? The day he feels like a man and wants to defend his mother.

He presses Play once more. We hear the voice of a little girl.

THE GIRL: Daddy!

THE FATHER: My daughter. . . Ulysses didn't have a daughter. (*He laughs.*) She's the only person of the female gender with whom I have a good relationship. My darling little girl. She is so beautiful, so intelligent, so. . . You don't believe my little girl shows her panties to boys, do you? I think that crazy woman is projecting. My daughter, my princess. . . (*He returns to sit down at the table.*) How I would have liked to kiss her tonight, my princess. How I would have liked us to eat altogether. How I would have liked to come home early enough to eat something warm, to have dinner as a family, in the light of day, and in the midst of my children's raucous play. I would have liked us to be a nice, normal family. Or a family of fools, even, lapping at an insipid broth in harmony. A normal family with a normal father, who might have slept with the nymphomaniac teacher, but who would have forgotten it all as soon as he crossed the threshold of his house. I would have liked. . .

He bursts into sobs.

NARRATOR: Paths crossing. This is the story of a man walking the streets of a city. The story of a man who crosses another man path on a street in a city. Two men who cross paths and don't stop.

THE FATHER: I can't take it any more! This heterosexual patriarch's disguise is more and more suffocating. But I don't know how to take it off, nor do I know what's underneath. What would this clandestine life look like, this life which I claim is the truth, without the fake one, the official one, to give it a rhythm and a frame? I can't take lying anymore, but I don't know where the lie is situated, exactly. One day it will all break apart. I already feel my face cracking, my odor betraying me. One day, the children will notice what's underneath. They will choose for me. Maybe they will tell me they love me and take me in their arms. Maybe not. There will be nothing left for me in the end. Except. . .

He presses Play on the tape recorder. We hear the little girl.

THE GIRL: Daddy!

Blackout.

III – CHILDREN

A child's bedroom, very messy. There is a hole the size of a fist in the back wall. Behind the wall, a violent argument is raging.

The boy and the girl are sitting on a large bed. They are dressed in matching big white t-shirts which reach down to their knees. They have their hands on their ears.

After several seconds, the sounds of the argument stop and the little girl removes her hands from her ears.

THE GIRL: There, I think they're done.

The boy removes his own hands from his ears.

They look at each other and smile.

The argument starts again. They cover their ears again and close their eyes.

THE BOY: Go plug up the hole!

The girl stands, picks up an enormous cork plug from the ground and plugs the hole, which largely muffles the noise.

When she returns to the bed, the boy begins to tickle her, laughing.

THE GIRL: (*Also laughing*) Stop! Stop! They'll come in!

THE BOY: They're arguing. They can't hear us.

THE GIRL: Stop!

He tickles her again, then stops suddenly and signals her to be quiet.

There is no more noise coming from the adjoining room.

THE BOY: They've stopped shouting. I bet they're crying now. Go see.

The girl stands again, removes the plug.

THE BOY: They're done.

THE GIRL: Do you think they heard us?

THE BOY: Of course not.

THE GIRL: Do you think they were arguing about us?

THE BOY: Yes.

THE GIRL: Because of the teacher?

THE BOY: No. Because of mom. That witch! She's jealous.

THE GIRL: Mom?

THE BOY: She's mad because she can't read our thoughts.

They look each other in the eyes for a few seconds, then burst into laughter.

THE GIRL: No!

THE BOY: Come on!

THE GIRL: Absolutely not.

THE BOY: Why?

THE GIRL: What if they heard us?

THE BOY: If they heard us, they'd say we're little pigs. And they'd send me to a reform school.

THE GIRL: You, to a reform school?

THE BOY: Yup.

THE GIRL: And not me?

THE BOY: No. They know nothing about justice, about fairness, about anything.

THE GIRL: Nothing about. . .

THE BOY: But they want us to know obedience and order.

The girl laughs.

THE BOY: They're irrational and naïve. (*He takes a cigarette and a lighter from his pocket and starts to smoke.*) And most of all, they're completely overwhelmed with their own problems.

THE GIRL: What, you're smoking? You shouldn't smoke. We shouldn't misbehave. If we misbehave, if we're not a-dor-a-ble, they'll want to get rid of us.

THE BOY: (*Smoking*) Dad already got rid of us.

THE GIRL: That's not true!

THE BOY: Yes it is! In his own way. . .

He takes out the tape recorder from under his bed.

THE GIRL: Oh! That's Dad's! You stole it!

The boy presses Play.

The voice of THE BOY on the tape recorder: Daddy, I'm so happy! So hap–

He presses OFF and throws the tape recorder on the ground.

THE BOY: Bullshit!

The girl picks it up, looks at it, then places it back on the ground delicately.

THE GIRL: And Mom. . . maybe she'll also want to abandon us.

THE BOY: Nah, abandon us where?

The girl thinks.

THE GIRL: In the woods. With wild animals: wolves, rhinos. So they can rip open our bellies.

THE BOY: Of course not! Wolves and rhinos don't even exist. You shouldn't believe fairytales, my love. If Mom abandons us, we'll simply drop pebbles along the path and come back home.

THE GIRL: And if she looses track of us again. If she's more sneaky the second time. If she lets us loose in the city. If she sells us to the city's animals: the pimps, the child-murderers. . . so that they rape us, slash up our faces and piss on us.

The boy crushes his cigarette on the floor.

THE BOY: Who taught you that, pimp? It wasn't me. Don't use words I haven't taught you. You don't know how to use them.

THE GIRL: What is a pimp, a p-i-m-p, if it's not what I said? (*She waits for his response.*) Oh! You don't know! Liar! I'm hungry.

THE BOY: You should have finished your plate instead of copying me just to make Mom angry.

THE GIRL: Aren't you hungry? And, by the way, what will we do for food in the city?

THE BOY: We'll buy food with money, of course! We'll just have to work. We'll just have to be. . . whores!

The girl appears very shocked and puts her hand over her mouth.

THE GIRL: Oh! Pimp! Pimp!

She throws herself on him, laughing.

They hit each other with pillows, laughing, and playing whore and pimp.

Suddenly, the girl stands and goes to the door of the room, at the back.

THE GIRL: I heard a door slam. He must have left.

THE BOY: So she'll go lock herself in her room. And we'll have the house to ourselves. Can I see your panties?

The girl hesitates. Finally, she lifts her t-shirt quickly.

THE BOY: I didn't see anything! Slower!

THE GIRL: Oh! And Mommy?

THE BOY: Don't worry. She's crying in bed. She's forgotten us.

She does it again more slowly.

THE BOY: That's the most beautiful thing in the world!

The girl laughs.

THE BOY: You promise you won't show them to anyone else?

THE GIRL: Of course not! Who do you think I am?

THE BOY: Liar!

THE GIRL: I swear.

The boy places his hands around her neck.

THE BOY: Liar! You already showed them to your classmates.

THE GIRL: Not these! Not my white panties!

The boy lets go of his sister's neck. He takes her in his arms.

THE BOY: I want you to be mine alone.

THE GIRL: I am yours alone.

THE BOY: No, I'm yours alone! I'm the one who's known you since you were born. I'm the one who was waiting for you before you were born. I can read your thoughts. I share your games, your sleep, your blood. I'm the only one who's loved you forever and will love you forever. Can I touch?

THE GIRL: No. It's not allowed.

THE BOY: Looking wasn't allowed either.

THE GIRL: Touching's less allowed than looking. Touching is e-x-p-l-i-

THE BOY: Stop spelling out words with X's as if you were a grown up. It's really dumb.

THE GIRL: No touching is explicitly mentioned in the law.

THE BOY: That law is stupid. They can't stand each other anymore but according to the law, they should touch. They don't love each other anymore but according to the law, they should have children. They complain about the law non-stop but they say it's for our benefit. They say I would hurt you! They're the ones who do all the hurting!

THE GIRL: They know more about love and about what might hurt us. And about who touches who.

A crash of objects and furniture comes from the adjoining room.

THE BOY: Will they ever shut up?

He hits the wall.

THE GIRL: Stop hitting! Stop!

THE BOY: They should hear us, at least a little! You think I'm afraid of them?

He hits again.

The girl goes to listen at the hole.

THE BOY: Is he back?

THE GIRL: No. It's Mom, alone. She's crying. Oh! (*She listens carefully.*) No, she's not crying.

She presses her ear to the hole.

THE GIRL: Oh! I think she's talking in her sleep. It's funny. (*She laughs.*) She says. . .

Suddenly she moves away from the door, her face ashen.

THE BOY: What? What is she saying?

The girl starts to cry.

THE BOY: For god sake, what? Why are you crying again?

THE GIRL: It's horrible!

THE BOY: What did she say, for fuck sake?

THE GIRL: (*Sobbing*) She says we're too old to sleep in the same bed. She says we need to be separated. Like at Mamie's. (*She runs and curls up on the bed, sobbing even harder.*) I don't want us to be separated!

THE BOY: Stop crying. Do you really think they can separate us? They can't.

THE GIRL: (*Still in tears*) Mommy said. . .

THE BOY: (*Mockingly*) Mommy said. Mommy decreed. Mommy ordered. (*To her*) But we say no. We are starting a rebellion. We are leaving.

THE GIRL: Leaving? You mean leaving our bed? Leaving our room?

THE BOY: Leaving the room and the house. Leaving our parents.

THE GIRL: Leaving our parents? Oh no, I'm scared!

THE BOY: Chicken. With me, you have nothing to fear.

THE GIRL: Are you sure? We're going outside? Leaving the city? Going. . . to Patagonia?

The boy sits on the bed and takes his sister in his arms.

The cries of the girl transform little by little into laughs, and her fear into enthusiasm.

THE BOY: We're not going to Patagonia. We're going further!

THE GIRL: To Siberia?

THE BOY: Further, even further!

THE GIRL: To Australia?

THE BOY: Not to Australia, my love. To paradise!

THE GIRL: To paradise? Oh yes! And can we go on a sled?

THE BOY: If you want.

THE GIRL: Pulled by German Shepherds.

They leap out of the bed.

Blackout.

NARRATOR: There is a sled by the door. The boy whistles and twelve German Shepherds come running in. The children harness them. They travel for a long time, to a country where laws reflect them. As soon as they arrive, they do what in the other world is a transgression and in paradise, is allowed.

Lights up on the same very messy room. On the back wall, a plank is nailed in and covers the hole. The children are now wearing a prince and a princess costume.

The girl is lying on the bed, in the position of a woman in labour. She yells.

The boy is opposite her like a midwife.

THE GIRL: Aaahhh!

THE BOY: Push! Push! Push!

THE GIRL: Aaahhh! Aaah!

With a final ripping scream, the girl gives birth to a stuffed rat.

The boy takes it in his arms and kisses it.

THE BOY: Oh! beautiful baby!

The girl smiles, her eyes are closed, she reaches her arms out to take the baby.

He gives it to her.

She takes it, opens her eyes and yells as soon as she sees it.

THE GIRL: It's a rat!

She stands and throws the rat across the room.

The boy picks it up and strokes it.

THE BOY: No, it's our baby. Look how handsome he is!

THE GIRL: It's gross. Get that thing out of my sight!

She starts to cry.

The boy sighs and throws the rat away.

THE BOY: There. Done.

The girl crosses her arms.

THE BOY: Come on, don't sulk. Let's just try again!

THE GIRL: Right now. I want a baby right now.

THE BOY: OK, right now. Let's go back to bed!

They lie down under the covers, side by side, looking straight ahead.

THE BOY: Now we make love.

THE GIRL: OK.

THE BOY: I love you.

THE GIRL: I love you too.

THE BOY: I love you!

THE GIRL: I love you too.

THE BOY: I love you!

THE GIRL: I love. . . Oh! I feel it coming. My stomach hurts.

THE BOY: The baby!

THE GIRL: Aaaah! My stomach hurts!

THE BOY: It's normal. You're in labor.

THE GIRL: Aaah! Why would this be normal? I thought we got rid of their rules. I thought everything that hurt in their world didn't exist here. Ah, it hurts!

THE BOY: (*Padding her forehead*) I don't know! Try to be brave!

THE GIRL: Aaaah! I thought our world was perfect!

THE BOY: It is!

THE GIRL: Aaah! I thought it was fair.

THE BOY: Fair and just!

THE GIRL: So why am I the one that's always in pain! Aaaaah! Aaaah! There it is! It's coming out. (*She sighs.*) You look. I'm too scared.

The boy slides under the covers.

THE BOY: (*Under the cover*) This time it's very pretty, you'll like it.

THE GIRL: Quick! I want to see.

The boy comes out from under the covers, a red rose in his hand.

THE BOY: Congratulations my love! It's not a rat!

THE GIRL: (*Taking the rose and smelling it*) But it's not a baby either! It smells good.

THE BOY: This rose is perfect. We don't need a baby.

The girl gets out of the bed and walks, looking lost.

The boy looks for a cigarette and a lighter. He smokes in bed.

THE BOY: What are you doing?

THE GIRL: Nothing.

THE BOY: Come!

She joins him.

There is a knock at the door.

The girl straightens up.

THE MOTHER's voice, very far away: Supper is ready, darlings! Come to the table!

The girl looks towards the door, then looks at her brother.

The boy seems not to have heard.

THE BOY: Kiss me!

He takes her in his arms.

They kiss.

THE BOY: Did you like it?

THE GIRL: Yes.

THE BOY: Good!

They kiss again.

There is another knock at the door.

The girl jumps up and moves away from her brother.

THE BOY: What's wrong?

THE GIRL: Did you hear?

THE BOY: Hear what? Are we kissing or what?

Distant voice of THE MOTHER: I said, supper is ready! Supper is ready, you little bastards. I'm going to loose it!

THE GIRL: She's going to loose it.

The boy goes back to smoking.

We hear the sounds of objects falling and of knives being sharpened.

THE GIRL: I'm scared

THE BOY: Why? I love you. We have every right. Here, you can do anything you want. Smoke, burn, fuck, break everything, rip everything open, repair everything.

The girl takes off her princess costume. She is left in her long white t-shirt. She approaches the back wall and presses her ear up to the place where the hole used to be.

THE GIRL: They're talking about us.

THE BOY: Who? The two assholes? They don't exist any more.

THE GIRL: They're talking about us. They're making fun of us. They say we're. . .

THE BOY: What? We're what?

THE GIRL: Sterile.

THE BOY: (*Smoking*) Sterile? Ste-rile. (*He laughs.*) Stop using words I didn't teach you. You're ridiculous.

THE GIRL: (*Still listening*) They say we have to go back. We have to go back.

He doesn't react, still smoking.

She straightens up and waits for him to react.

THE BOY: Come to bed, stupid! You'll catch a cold. (*Pause*) Come!

THE GIRL: I'm going back. I'm taking the sled.

She turns towards the door.

THE BOY: Where are you going? You're not going anywhere! (*He throws the cigarette, runs towards his sister and grabs her by the throat.*) We can't go back to the house, stupid. After what we've done, it's no longer possible.

Distant voice of THE MOTHER: (*On top of the sound of knives being sharpened*) Supper, darlings! Mommy loves you!

THE GIRL: I want to go home! Let me go home!

THE BOY: You're looking for trouble? Huh? You want Mom to cut our throats?

Distant voice of THE MOTHER: (*On top of the sound of footsteps and knives being sharpened*) My little girl! My darling girl!

THE GIRL: Daddy... Daddy won't let her. Daddy will protect us.

THE BOY: Bullshit! You're messing everything up.

He squeezes her neck, shakes her.

She lets him do it, inert.

At last, he stops strangling her and takes her in his arms. He kisses her. He laughs.

THE BOY: You're so pretty! Oh, look! You have breasts!

She doesn't respond, frozen.

He releases her and shouts.

THE BOY: Damn it! Don't mess everything up!

THE GIRL: We don't know how to do this. Nothing grows here, don't you see? I'm leaving.

THE BOY: Shit!

He goes and curls up on the bed.

THE BOY: You're stupid! You're a cheater! You're breaking your promise!

The noises from outside finally subside.

THE GIRL: I'm packing.

THE BOY: And I'm left here, like a dumbass! I'm left here like a dumbass!

THE GIRL: I'm . . .

She leaves the room and returns with a huge suitcase.

The boy jumps up.

THE BOY: No! Let me do it!

He tears the suitcase from her hands.

THE GIRL: You want. . .

THE BOY: Let me do it!

He takes off his prince costume and is in his big white t-shirt again.

THE BOY: I'll also pack some flowers and a huge diamond, so you know I forgive you.

He picks through the mess of the room and finds a bouquet of plastic flowers and a giant fake plastic diamond.

THE GIRL: Thank you. You're kind. You're. . .

THE BOY: And I'll pack a little piece of me, I'll cut out an eye, or cut off a finger. . .

THE GIRL: No! Stop! We're done!

THE BOY: I'll do it, I'm telling you! I'll do it and I'll put it there, among your shirts. Because without you I'm disabled. And this way you'll always remember me.

THE GIRL: Don't say that. Someone will come, you know. For you. A woman. One day. You'll heal.

The boy places the suitcase on the bed, opens it. He packs the flowers and the diamond. Then he collects objects and clothes here and there, and places them in the suitcase, all while continuing to speak.

THE BOY: I'm packing your suitcase but let me warn you. Without me you'll be an exile, a stray, a prostitute. You'll walk alone and you'll get lost. You'll give yourself to strangers. You'll be hungry. You'll be cold. You'll get sick and you'll cough up blood. You'll be ripped into pieces by wildcats' claws. You'll be snacked on by wolves. And someone will see you: lost, frozen and starving, so he'll take you in. He'll promise to love you, but he'll tear you apart. He'll promise to marry you but he'll enslave you. He'll promise to believe you but he'll judge you. He'll promise to forgive you, but he'll abandon you. He'll promise to wait for you, but he'll sleep with women, he'll sleep with men. He'll promise to stay, but he'll leave with women, he'll leave with men. He'll promise to always look at you, but he'll close his eyes, saying you've gotten old. He'll promise to remember, but he'll sink into amnesia.

When he stops talking, the suitcase is ready and contains all the objects which were strewn across the floor of the room and on the bed, except the prince and princess costumes.

During what follows, the parents' dialogue is heard softly in the background, at the same time as the children's.

THE GIRL: She'll be very beautiful, the woman.

THE BOY: I don't care. I hate her.

THE GIRL: She'll love you.

THE BOY: Stay.

THE GIRL: No, you go back with me. We can go back. They haven't noticed what we've done. We are still welcome there.

THE BOY: Go back like losers, no thank you

THE GIRL: Come with me.

The boy doesn't move.

The girl turns away.

The boy turns his back to her. He screams, as if he were really cutting off some part of his body, which he then places in the suitcase.

The girl looks at him, horrified.

THE BOY: It's ready.

THE GIRL approaches him and puts her hand on his shoulder.

He keeps his back turned.

Distant voice of THE FATHER: You are beautiful.

Distant voice of THE MOTHER: Telepathy. You said we had a telepathic connection.

Distant voice of THE FATHER: You are beautiful, my love

Distant voice of THE MOTHER: I'm pregnant.

Distant voice of THE FATHER: Our paths just crossed. It won't happen again.

Distant voice of THE MOTHER: Why are you back so late? We can't reverse course. Why won't you look at me? Answer me. Answer me. Answer me. Answer me. Answer me. Answer me. Answer me. Answer me. Answer me.

Distant voice of THE FATHER: Our paths crossed. These are the ramifications.

Distant voice of THE MOTHER: Answer me!

Distant voice of THE FATHER: It's a family. It's such a beautiful tree.

THE GIRL: The woman... tell her that you mutilated yourself. She'll think you did it for her and everything will be OK.

The girl takes the suitcase.

THE BOY: (*Back still turned*) You'll remember what I told you.

THE GIRL: Everything will be alright, my love.

The girl exits, suitcase in hand.

The boy remains alone.

The lights dim slowly.

Distant voice of THE MOTHER: Answer me!

Distant voice of THE FATHER: My children.

Distant voice of THE MOTHER: Answer me!

Distant voice of THE FATHER: My children.

Distant voice of THE MOTHER: Answer me!

Distant voice of THE FATHER: My children! My children! My children...

Children's voices are heard, laughing and crying

CHILD'S VOICE: Daddy!

Final Blackout.

LADJABLÈS-WILD WOMAN
by
Daniely Francisque

MARTINIQUE

translation by Danielle Carlotti-Smith

Characters:

MAN

WOMAN

THE MASK

VOICE

This text was created on January 19, 2018 at the Tropiques Atrium National Theater of Martinique, featuring a set by the author, with Rita Ravier and Patrice Turlet (actors), Max Diakok (choreography), Marcel Jean-Baptiste (music), Viviane Vermignon (lights), Fred Lagnau (video), Melissa Simon-Hartman and Sylviane Gody (costumes).

The range of three acts in three symbolic colors has been inspired by the ritual of Carnival in Martinique, from Fat Tuesday (red) until Ash Wednesday (black and white).

Prologue

VOICE: They say that she's a Night Creature who appears at high noon. That she shows up alone at festivities, on the side of the road or on the riverbanks. They say her mesmerizing beauty inflames everyone's desire. They say she is a fearsome seductress who relentlessly enslaves men to her charms without mercy, dragging them in her wake to their ultimate death, somewhere, at the foot of a cliff. They say that beneath the long dress she wears that outlines her voluptuous curves, she conceals a hoof. Woe betide anyone who discovers it. He shall lose his soul.

Red

Night of Carnival. Rhythmic music.
Alone on a city sidewalk, a man wearing a costume, and a half mask on his face.

VOICE: Ladies and gentleman, there he was a poor-devil in the midst of a throng of people dancing. A man who cried with no tears, who laughed without joy, who lived without heart. But no one saw it. Not even him. And no one gave a damn. Neither did he. His two shining eyes had long been sightless, and his living-body had long been a walking-corpse that never felt the slightest pain. He didn't give a damn, I tell you. That day, our man had sung-danced-cussed under a shower of confetti carried by the colorful-masked-costumed wave of carnival, which come nightfall, had vomited him like a drunk onto the sidewalks of the jubilant city.

MAN: *Siwo!* I am syrop-man!
To try him is to taste him, to taste him is to savor him, and to savor him is to miss him already!
You can munch on the earth's crust, taste the bark of men, but you won't find a hotter, more beautiful, more coconut-crystal specimen than this here sweet-syrup man. . .

My brown sugar body doesn't contain a single grain of salt, 6 feet tall, one hundred percent original, for my father was honey, my mother caramel, and I was born under the shade of a cinnamon sky, between the udders of an eternal hour.

I am a man who delights in constant tasting, and find no need to enter into negotiation or stroll down the boulevard of passion in order to crash into you, dear, no, just one look from me puts you in ebullition and sows confusion in your emotions. . .

Look out! M'lady damsels and virginal dames, my erogenous zone is a rebel with supernatural powers! Take heed when touching it in order to avoid an explosion and the pleasure of immoderate consumption.

And I'm hungry! I'm hungering for a virgin to devour in strips, craving a little candy to cling to my taste buds, hankering for the flesh of a hibiscus to coat with my syrup, hungering for some woman's sugar to devour-digest-defecate!

Siwo! Sticky-sweet man to sip and swirl around in your mouth! To try him is to taste him, to taste him is to savor him, and to savor him is to miss him already!

VOICE: Ladies and gentlemen, this is the story of a drunken fool, a hungry fool, who didn't want to be on his own one evening during carnival. He had danced, gesticulated, raised hell in all the streets of town, and even though the masked flock had since moved on, loneliness had continued to well up inside him. My man was there looking out into the void, striding along the deserted streets, wolf-whistling all the well-rounded silhouettes on his path on his search for a solitary damsel to take with him, and that's when. . .

An apparition. In high heels, a woman dressed in flaming red, her face covered by a mask.

MAN: There. There she is.
   I tell you, I see her, over there.
   A romantic little wisp of a woman
   with skin the color of a sapodilla tree
   and a mouth like a mandarin.

   There,

   Nostrils flared, I already
   inhale her scent, there,
   fragrance of a girl-in-solitude,
   of a girl in need of love,
   of a girl in need of lust.

   There,

   I'm already salivating
   I salivate and erupt
   my weapons of easy seduction,

I deploy my desire
and I pounce on the pretty girl.

TACTIC #1: NEUTRALIZE THE TARGET

One: identify the target. Without frightening the damsel, take aim with my compulsive testosterone. Notice how she wanders, how she daydreams, blissfully unaware that I'm closing in on her. . .

Two: arm yourself. Polish one of my pheromone bullets to inflame her passion. That's it, hang on there, baby. In a moment, your life will be changed forever. . .

Three: fire! Plant my projectile-desire in the retina of the sweet and sour dreams streaming from your pupils. *Pow!*

Bing! I blast my fake smile.
Bo! I spray her with my synthetic bedroom eyes.
Pla! Throw her three or four mystical flashes, and immediately notice that my prey is surprised and even moved, indeed, I see that she is convulsing and that her wild pelt shivers. . .

Boom! Here comes the fatal blow, advance with a triumphal walk and with a royal gesture seize the doll whose breath is riddled with moans.

Target captured.

TACTIC #2: MAKE HER DRINK THE RAINBOW

Ladies and gentlemen, observe how for her I become a man who is heaven-sent, who has fallen from the sky with my sugar syrup honey. See how my crazy coconut sugar becomes existential in this sacrificial ritual.

MAN: Good evening.

WOMAN: Good evening.

MAN: How about a drink?

WOMAN: Why not...

MAN: Zombie-Syrup cocktail? A radiance to her gaze, a sliver of laughter, a shard of sound, and she says...

WOMAN: Yes.

MAN: Too easy. As a practical man, I race to the bar and with my ten agile fingers I perform my magic trick. *Abracadabrachoof!* A tiny drop of venom in a rainbow cocktail, a trap set for the lips of the damsel with the never-ending smile. And I say to her, "Here you go...". And she drinks, her lips kiss the cold glass as she drinks sexily, abundantly, slowly consuming the Obeah spell which without the slightest hint of violence, in just a moment will knock her out cold. She drinks while I elegantly distill the divine drip of my syrup-words in the butterfly of her ear.

(*He sings*.) Your eyes set me on fire baby
heat up my veins sweety
my heart is racing my *doudou* honey
like a thoroughbred in my chest
it's no joke baby
your fatal beauty kills me
Tonight you'll be the Queen of my Carnival
and I will be your stallion *doudou* darling
so mount my goddess, come now don't be shy
together tonight we will ride
and blablabla!...

As a good lover, joker, and ladies' man, I run the show as she laughs and she warms up, laughs and sips, laughs without knowing that little by little I'm making her fall asleep. She laughs, laughs, laughs, which makes the stars in her eyes shine all the more.

But suddenly, her pupils
Her precious glittering pupils twitch within the retina and then flicker.
Suddenly, the flame.
The flame in her pupils wavers and gently expires within the almond gaze of her distress.
All of a sudden Beauty

Beauty with the faded pupils stumbles and collapses in the arms of Prince Charming, eyelids closed and body hypnotized. . .

Target hit.

TACTIC # 3: EMBARK ON A MISSION

Sleep, fruit-flavored princess, sleep with your whole body,
I hunger for your body but not your gaze, sleep,
Like an impulsive octopus, let me palpate the pulp of your mango body, epicurean pulp, pulp of the angels.

Sleep, sugar doll, let those two eyes of yours slumber,
I hunger for your body but not your tenderness, sleep,
For there is nothing better than your empty body
In which to unload the bitterness of a lost man.

Sleep. No need to fall for me, fall in love or shudder,
Sleep. No need to open yourself or offer yourself like a flower unfurling,
Sleep. Showing no remorse, it is I who peel away your body's outer layer, and without your permission, peck and devour you, and thus dissipate myself.

Sleep, candid Princess with stars in your eyes, sleep,
let me perform my phenomenal ferocity solo,
secretly invade your horizontal anatomy,
allow me to embark as a missionary to colonize your beautiful jewels,
and like an infidel profane the constellations on your skin.

Sleep, sleep deeply, until tomorrow, until dawn.
and when just before daybreak the Gray Kingbird sings *piripiri*,
when you part the curtains of your numbed eyelids,
I, your incubus, your *dorlis*, your night zombie,
I, the vagabond will have long since taken leave.

I will have left without a gesture, without a caress.
Evaporated without so much as leaving an address,
having nevertheless discharged in your violated interior
the venomous trace of my poisonous syrup.

Poison from a bad seed,
poison like gangrene,
larval lifeblood that in nine lunar revolutions
will sow misfortune between your bitter sides
your forbidden fruit, face of night,
crownless fruit, with no roots or heritage,
pitifully grown among your screaming rage.

Siwo! I'm the syrup-man,
Soulless sniper, ravisher of women,
Male-papaya planter of orphan fruit,
pounded by pelvic thrusts to stolen wombs.

Mine are the ladyloves ready to be sniffed!
Mine are the heady hibiscuses ready to make me swoon!
Mine are all the chicks ready to plunge me into ecstasy!
Mine are all the gazelles ready to intoxicate me!

Siwo, sweet-sugar man to deal on the street!
Sugar-man to pimp out!
Sugarcane-man to intoxicate!
To try him is to. . .

The masked woman imposes herself before him.

MAN: Hey there my princess. . . you. . . you're not asleep. . . ?

WOMAN: Surprise attack!

The woman seizes him and kisses him hard, leaving the man stunned. Then in a single gesture, she activates the music and starts dancing in a wild and frenzied manner.

MAN: Ladies and gentleman, there I was like an emasculated macho, like an unpunished junkie, there I tell you, like a plucked rooster.
A red tigress who appeared out of nowhere had just kissed me, the unarmed hunter, with her red hot pepper mouth. She set my eternal night ablaze. No woman before her, not one, I tell you, had ever. . .

He approaches the masked woman.

MAN: Woah! Audacious princess. Smoldering princess. Are you provoking me or am I dreaming? Did you just take my lips?

WOMAN: . . .

MAN: You dance like a goddess, you know? I see sparks fly from your black heels. What is the little name that honors you, flamboyant princess?

WOMAN: . . .

MAN: Maryàn? Caroline? No, tonight, I bet your name is. . . Touloulou. *Princess Touloulou* or *Lady Touloulou*, if you prefer.

WOMAN: . . .

MAN: Mh, are we playing mystery woman? It's true that the touloulous are as secretive as hermit crabs. . . But you, my Princess, you are not like the rest of them, you didn't hide everything. . . I see your whole body, everything except your mysterious face. . . You're a real anatomical bomb, my Princess, has anyone ever told you that?

WOMAN: I'm not a princess.

The woman turns away.

MAN: Woah! You're leaving without saying goodbye? You are the Queen of the Savages, my word, the Queen of the Fierce. We could have calmly traded a few words, and gulped down a rainbow before saying bye-bye. Or not. You can stay with me, if you like. I'm sure the two of us could gave gotten along, the explosion of our laughter scattering around like confetti under the dark petticoat of the tropical night. We certainly could have flashed our bedroom eyes like fireflies in the skies of our desires, don't you think?

The woman continues past him silently.
He blocks her path.

Shouldn't play an uptight woman like that, doudou-honey. That cuts you off from others. When you're as charming as you are, you need to know how to be friendly. If only with a smile, by answering me when I speak to you, by laughing, reacting or roaring?

WOMAN: . . .

MAN: She isn't responding. But when the door to a woman's lips stays closed like that, it's not that she doesn't want to answer or that she's not interested. What she really wants is for you to keep sweet talking her.

Aii! You're breaking my back and my heart, you're killing me, I'm at the edge of my grave, you know, like a rotting jackfruit.

Unresponsive, the woman continues to walk.

Hey, I'm talking to you. Couldn't my words at least send a shiver up your spine? My syrup-words soften your heart of stone? And my *colatura* loosen the cadence of your steps?

But nothing?. . . Can't you even make puppy dog eyes at me? . . . You're so uptight. As unwavering as an unforgiving bolt of lightning tearing up the solitary night sky. As unrelenting as the sadness hanging from the tip of the despairing branch of a tree.

The woman continues walking.

MAN: Woah! When you walk by me like that, ooo! It's a heavenly sight, a walking aphrodisiac that could turn the sleepiest man into an insomniac. . . Your body is a landscape, sweetie. When I look at you, I travel, become a nomad traversing your panoramic body. I climb your insurmountable mountains, leap from waterfall to waterfall, and plunge into the lunar flow of your rivers. I dream of wrapping myself in the cocoon of your caves to recover in the lower back of the world.

Imagine this. You in me, me in you, body-to-body,
our beads of sweat dripping down the melted wings of time,
our fever burning up the loins of the night,
our lips coiled after the storm of our cries,
Let's leave now, sugar, let's ride to paradise,
Start by removing your mask so I can see your beautiful moon face.

The woman continues walking in silence.

Ah! Stop keeping your tongue to yourself, honey, it makes me crave it! Come, my sugar, come to me so I can make you melt on my teeth. The party is now a world away, there is no one who will stumble upon us there among the trees. Take off your mask, together we'll be fine.

The woman speeds up. He trots behind her.

Ah, gentlemen! Trying to engage with this woman was as difficult a challenge as climbing the tallest mountain backwards! I walked and walked so much that I ended up walking 'round in circles over and over again. And during that time, I chewed over my useless words until they fell apart, and at no time did the heartless wench drop me a single verbal breadcrumb.

Hey! Tiger-Queen, I've been talking to you for a while, but my words evaporate like smoke on the nape of your neck, am I not good enough for you? There you are walking by me rolling your hips like that, without a word, not even the tiniest word, not even a display of courtesy, not even a swear word to the jerk who's trailing you. It's disdainful. Yes, disdainful. So go hang yourself in the deep asshole of the night! As for me, I'm getting out of here! Rotting bitch of a woman!

The man walks away grumbling to himself.

What? You think I'm going to walk around following her like this all night long? Here I am begging like a dog, like a beggar? I guess I got no pride left? I may be a jerk, but I'm not a moron!

He stops in his tracks, and turns around.

Wait a second. . . Don't tell me you're. . . married?. . . Married! . . . Ah, so that's what it is, *madame* is married and she now under curfew! Yeah, after dancing depravedly and arousing a stallion-man all evening long, Queen Touloulou is now feeling guilty and is rushing home to her prison before the stroke of midnight?. . . But it's carnival, sugar, there's no schedule and anything goes. Forget about your husband and at zero o'clock on the dot, you'll be my mare and I'll be your stallion, and tomorrow all will be forgotten. Simply, properly, discretely. Between two trees, on a carpet of leaves, let's do it, the forest is a just a little beyond, let's go, honey. . .

The man approaches slowly and tries to kiss her.
Suddenly, a clap of thunder, night fades.

Black

Deep in the forest, where four paths intersect, the man is lying down. A huge white moon punctures the black sky.
Above him stands the woman who fixes him with her gaze.

MAN: Hey, wait, wait, wait, what's going on?. . . What the hell are we doing here? A second ago we were on the road, and now we're. . . ?

WOMAN: Shut up.

MAN: Excuse me. . . ?

WOMAN: You talk too much.

MAN: What. . . You're talking?

WOMAN: Get undressed now.

MAN: What?

WOMAN: Your costume, take it off.

MAN: No.

WOMAN: I said take it off.

MAN: I'll take my clothes off if I want to.

WOMAN: So why do you think I've brought you here?

MAN: You didn't bring me anywhere, I'm the one who. . . What, you. . . you brought me here on purpose?

WOMAN: I want you.

MAN: You want me ? After all that silence, you want. . . ?

WOMAN: Take everything off.

MAN: I got it. You turn me on, you escape. I follow you, you flee. I talk to you, you ignore me. All of that to make my temperature rise and hook me to the line of desire. You're on fire, you are. Let me see that volcano hidden under your dress.

WOMAN: Stay away.

MAN: You're cruel, you make me boil over.

WOMAN: Not yet.

MAN: Naughty little thing, you want me to do a little striptease, and you'll be watching behind your mask? Take it off, I want to see your face.

WOMAN: Not like this.

MAN: Why? We are two solitary forms beneath the moon, why should you hide? Do you wish to give me your body without your face.

WOMAN: I want you first.

MAN: Mh, you're driving me crazy. But by blowing so much on my fire, you may end up blowing it out. You brought me here for a reason, didn't you? So quit showing off.

WOMAN: Isn't it my body that you want? So offer yourself up for my pleasure. Entirely.

MAN: What about you? Aren't you offering anything? You're on a weird trip, there. You want it all, yet you give nothing. What you want you'll eventually get, you woman in heat.

WOMAN: You're the one who's getting what you wanted.

MAN: Are you provoking me? Look where you are. Alone in the woods with horny feral dog. Things could go badly, so stop provoking me.

WOMAN: Shut up. Take your clothes off and lie down there.

MAN: Woah! What kind of woman are you? A chick with balls, is that it? This new breed of women, who under the pretext of equality between the sexes, believes that she can do whatever she wants, and becomes the enemy of men to the point of castrating them in order to transplant their testicles between her thighs, like a war trophy? But what war, huh? For what? Why do you want balls between your legs since they are already well attached between ours?. . . If you want me to lie down, start by lying down.

WOMAN: What do you take me for, a garden that's just there to be planted? I don't need your seeds.

MAN: A provoker, that's what you are. You're putting a damper on things. There's nothing left for me to do here.

The man leaves. He gets lost again, and finds himself back in the same place. He tries to go in a different direction. He returns again. The woman sings an incantation.

MAN: Woah! What dreary path have you lead me on? I can't find my way back. Show me the way. . .

WOMAN: . . .

MAN: I said: Show me the way!

WOMAN: . . .

MAN: What? Have your ears closed up?

WOMAN: Path marked, path cut, all paths are paths.

MAN: I'm asking for my way.

WOMAN: Two paths criss-crossed, four paths cut, all paths are crossing.

MAN: Has the woman gone permanently insane?

WOMAN: Covered or uncovered, all paths are a mystery.

MAN: Woh! I'm getting out of here.

He leaves again, the path suddenly disappears. The man falls.

MAN : Hey you madwoman, let me go now!

WOMAN: Well, then, go on your way.

The woman bursts into disquieting laughter.

MAN: Does this nut job take me for a jerk? I've been running to the left and to the right, up and down, all paths look the same and bring me back to the same spot. Hey, is it you who dragged me here? Tell me how I can get out of here!

WOMAN: Where you going, little dude? The night is just beginning to get lighter.

MAN: A kidnapping. This is a kidnapping. You're kidnapping me, isn't that what you're doing? Help me! I'm a prisoner!

WOMAN: You're the one who followed me without being forced. You're the one who poured your syrup-words on my footsteps.

MAN: Alright, but now I want to get out of here, go back there, get myself off this trail for stray dogs.

WOMAN: Not like that.

MAN: What do you mean, *not like that?*

WOMAN: Start by finding the path.

MAN: Path? What path?

WOMAN: The one you need to cross in order to find your way.

MAN: Here she goes again!

WOMAN: There is only one path that will take you back to the place from which you came.

MAN: The place I came from? That's exactly where I want to go right now. Let me pass.

WOMAN: Not like that.

MAN: Dammit, who the hell told me to follow this lunatic? Here she is unspooling my brains! I find myself captive here, caught under a midnight sun blocked by a vertical wall of trees stretching as far as the dark side of the sky.

The woman unties her red clothes.

MAN: Hey, what are you doing? No. No. No. . . What are. . . No, what are you doing?

WOMAN: Wasn't it you who wanted to explore my landscape?

MAN: Not anymore. That's what I told you a little while ago, but I don't want to anymore.

WOMAN: You can't take back what you've already said.

MAN: Yes, alright. But I was caught up in the heat of the moment, you understand, the bacchanalian booze-infused, confetti-flying, festival of female flesh atmosphere. I followed you like a wild dog. But I was kidding around, festival fever made my tongue loose.

WOMAN: You should weigh your words carefully before you speak. If your man's words don't have any value it means you're worthless.

MAN: Hey, that's not a reason to disrespect me. Don't get carried away. You're not any better, you bloody bitch! You're the one who came along shaking your caboose under my nose, you're the one who got me all hot. You're the one who wants to unceremoniously undress me. And now you're the one telling me I'm worthless? Well, all you have to do is lie down there, you with your mask, and I'll show you if I'm worthless or not.

WOMAN: What, 4 inches?

MAN: 4 inches?

WOMAN: Do you calculate your value in terms of 4 inches of ticklish parts?

MAN: No 8. At least 8 inches.

WOMAN: Your famous "supernatural sensual zone"?

MAN: Lie down over there, I say, in a moment you won't be laughing.

WOMAN: Aren't you going to ask me to drink something first?

MAN: What?

WOMAN: Your rainbow poison?

MAN: No need to. I'll stick your mouth straight to the roots.

WOMAN: So you can take advantage of me like all the others?

MAN: To drown your eyes among the leaves.

WOMAN: Pathetic creep.

MAN: I'll break you, and steal your precious pearl, and you'll be off the rails by the break of day.

WOMAN: Pitiful syrup.

MAN: Yes, Syrup. I'm the Syrup-Man.
    I have honor, value, and all my vigor,
    and my 8 inches will silence you and make you quiver.

    I'll fold your undisciplined harridan's body,
    I'll sink my teeth into your red pepper flesh,
    and I'll tame your Spartacus-like ways,
    so that against your will I can colonize your uterus.

    Yes, Syrup. I'm the Syrup-Man.
    I have value, vigor, and all my pride,
    and the acidic poison that sets my loins ablaze inside,
    between your volcano rocks will lead to bloom
    the illegitimate fruit of my bitterness and gloom.

WOMAN: What is a sugar-man worth?
   What is the value of a masked man,
   a frustrated man, a victimized man?

   What is a lying-man worth?
   What is the value of a horror-man,
   a raping-man, a bad luck-man?

   What is a ravaged-man worth?
   A man without a face,
   without a shore,
   without an anchor?

   What is a desert-man worth?
   What is the value of a pipe-dream man,
   a cold-hearted man, a castrated-man?

MAN: Woah, hold on now. . .

WOMAN: Pathetic braggart. You think you're a hunter when in fact real hunters look their prey in the eye and tremble alongside them in the space of a moment.

MAN: Shut up!

WOMAN: No, what you are is a thief. You break into women's bodies. You take because you have nothing to give. You're empty. Your mouth is full of words. But your eyes are deserts, just like your existence, deserts; you don't know why you're alive. You sow the seeds of your own oblivion in the bellies of women out of fear that you'll disappear. But you don't exist. You're nothing. You're empty.

MAN: Shut up!

WOMAN: We are not eternal romantic victims.
   Not your angels, not your saints, not your prostitutes.
   We are not princesses who need to be rescued.
   Not your minx, not your monsters, or inferior objects.
   We are not just uterus for giving birth.
   Nor trophies, nor dolls, nor private property.

MAN: And you, who are you?!

WOMAN: I'm everything but your bird. So take off your rooster feathers. Have the balls to be a man.

MAN: Insolent woman, I'm going to smash your face. . .

Furious, the man rushes toward her.
In one magical gesture, the woman knocks him down and puts her foot on his chest.

WOMAN: Target knocked down.

MAN: Am I imaging things or did this woman just. . .

WOMAN: My name.

MAN: What?

WOMAN: Say my name.

MAN: But I don't know you.

WOMAN: You know who I am.

MAN: Me. . . I know you? Are you trying to tell me that we. . . , you and I, have already. . . ?

WOMAN: My name!

MAN: Tania, Laura, Mirella, Nadia, Ericka, Lala. . . ?

WOMAN: Keep trying.

MAN: Virginie, Sylvie, Magali, Stéphanie, Lily?. . . I don't know!

WOMAN: My mystery-name. I want my alias. Give me my wild woman name.

MAN: I don't know any wild women.

WOMAN: Then will stay here, trapped with me among these four dead-end paths.

The woman walks away.

MAN: How could I possibly know your name? Your face is hidden behind a mask. What is a masked-woman worth?

The woman stops. Removes her mask.

MAN: Now turn around. Let me see your ugly wild woman face.

She turns around and slowly lifts her dress, allowing her hoof to be seen. The man suddenly panics.

WOMAN: Where are you creeping away to, little man. . . ?

MAN: Back off! Go away! Go away!

WOMAN: Too late. I've already kidnapped you.

MAN: I said back off!. . . Three signs of the cross for protection, three signs of the cross for conjuration.

WOMAN: Tell me who I am. Give me my name, say it out loud.

MAN: No! You are the one. . . the one whose name should never be uttered.

WOMAN: Then you know who I am.

MAN: Back off!

WOMAN: Say my name, say it.

MAN: Never!

WOMAN: What? What happened to your syrupy superman balls?

MAN: Oh, guardian angels protect me, please. Back off, I said!. . .

WOMAN: Don't you know how to face your fear?

MAN: Back off!. . .

WOMAN: HAVE THE BALLS TO SAY MY NAME, DAMMIT, OR MAY A LIGHTENING BOLT SPLIT YOU IN TWO!

MAN: Djablès! Djablès! Your name is. . . You are the She-Devil. . .

WOMAN: Your lips summoned me. Now you are mine.

In a single movement, the She-Devil turns off the moon, which turns black against the white sky.
The man runs away, but keeps coming back, because all the paths lead to a dead end.

WOMAN: Djablès
    That's what they call me
    Djablès like an ogress
    like a tigress
    like vengefulness

    Djablès
    That's the name I've been given
    Djablès like Amazon
    like demon
    like pheromone

    Sorceress with eyes like embers
    nocturnal raptor roaring under the black moon
    I dig my sharpened talons
    into the wild flesh of your hidden desires

    Black Venus with the mysterious lips
    cannibal succubus of your sleep
    with my jagged fangs I gnaw
    the secret sap of your unconfessed fantasies

    Djablès
    That's what they call me

Djablès like adultery
like a powder keg
like millenary

Djablès
That's the name I've been given
Djablès like Lilith
Carmen Kali
Like Erzuli

And if you have the audacity to follow the swing of my hips
in search of a libertine promise of tenderness

If you are a man-dog obsessed with one obscene desire
who seeks to take down my moon to display it with your trophies on high

If you wish to push me down, discharge yourself before slipping away
to make your testicled-male pride prevail

Know that it is I who tied you to an invisible leash
I who pull you up to hallucinatory heights
like a *bwabwa* puppet you yourself play

Djablès
That's what they call me
Djablès like female
like rebel
like cruel

Djablès
That's the name I've been given
Djablès like wild
Implacable
Animal-woman

Djablès, three times your lips have said my name.
So here I am standing before your eyeballs.

VOICE: Ladies and gentlemen, he had nevertheless been forewarned, *stop chasing women as if they were prey, the djablès will end up taking you away*. But our man didn't believe those stories passed down from a time when dogs still barked from their tails. He wanted to continue to defy the universal laws of voracity. All of a sudden, there he is caught like a game bird, captured at darkest midnight by a formidable *djablès*, trapped like a victim among the four paths of a haunted forest.

MAN: I beg you, Queen Djablès, let me go.

WOMAN: You summon me and now you run away?

MAN: I wasn't looking for a woman like you.

WOMAN: Like *me*?

MAN: A monster who lures men only to devour them.

WOMAN: What better when faced with a monster who devours women?

MAN: Ah, no no, don't play with words, Djablès. You *really* devour them. They say that they are found dead or dismembered at the bottom of a cliff, or mysteriously evaporated; the luckiest ones have their brains unraveled. I have never killed anyone. As for you, you are a monster, a real monster.

WOMAN: It's been a long time since I appeared among men. They had relegated me to the gutter of their darkest fantasies. I was too desirable, but too indomitable, thus too monstrous. But if today I came out of the darkness, it's because you searched for me in the mire of your fear. So what is that you want ?

MAN: I don't want anything. I just want to get out of here.

WOMAN: No one can take their leave without making a sacrifice of some kind. All those who failed to follow this rule had their necks broken.

MAN: Dammit. Who told me to follow this demon? What an asshole I am!

WOMAN: The needle on your compass gets overworked by the swinging of my hips just by sight. . . Never have I captured anyone with such ease in the dead of night.

MAN: You. . . you. . . hypnotized me. Yes, hypnotized me. I wasn't myself.

WOMAN: On the contrary, you were exactly yourself.

MAN: Everyone knows who you are snake-woman. A charmer who enchants and disarms men. You possessed me. You blinded me.

WOMAN: And is that why your trembling?

MAN: No. If I'm trembling, it's because I'm cold.

WOMAN: That's a lie. Fear makes your virile members tremble.

MAN: I'm not afraid. Do you really believe that an old witch like you is going to make me. . . No, don't get so close. Why did you drag that damn hoof of yours over to me what do you really want get off my path chimera-woman go die in the mire of your backward deformity I said animal woman bitch woman horse you have the devil in your body no *you are the devil* the devil can only be a louse of an unholy woman like you a real dirty you woman you're nothing but blood and bone and hooves monster a harlot with a stinking pussy who rides men to better devour them between her thighs you deform the world damn woman disfigure men stop defying me with your look full of flames do you want to devour me as well what are you thinking you think that you aren't. . .

WOMAN: Kiss me.

MAN: . . .

WOMAN: Kiss me.

MAN: I must wake up. This woman is a nightmare. . .

WOMAN: Kiss me.

MAN: This sky is unreal. Wake me up!

WOMAN: You want to leave this place without me tearing out your brain?

MAN: Yes, I'm counting on leaving with my brain intact.

WOMAN: Then you must give me a kiss.

MAN: You already stole a kiss earlier, that should suffice. Your mouth is a fire. My lips can still recall. No, I don't want to.

WOMAN: This time it's up to you to kiss me. I won't steal a kiss from you. Give it to me.

MAN: Never!

WOMAN : Look at me. Give-it-to-me.

MAN: Stop. . . your eyes. . . they're devouring me. . .

WOMAN: Come closer. Kiss me, let my lips set your fear on fire.

MAN: No, I can't do it.

The MAN *is attracted despite himself.*

WOMAN: Come closer. Let me make you, you cheap puppet of a man, soar. Come. Let the tongue of my flames devour your grotesque bacchanalian man's mask.

MAN: I'm so cold. . .

WOMAN: Come. Kiss my burning lips. Remove your plumed costume. Come closer. Allow your costumed man's skin to be consumed. Come. Let my fire bite you down to the bone, to the shell of your lies. Come a little closer. Come here so my lips can set your abyss aflame. . .

Irresistibly, the man kisses the djablès. Suddenly suffocating, the man struggles with his mask.

In a cloud of noise, voices are raised, fused, and curse from all directions.

THE MASK: Danm! Quit crying like a young girl!
    Danm! Quit crying like a young girl!
    A woman with desire is a vampire.
    I said your father doesn't exist.
    Woman is the door through which the devil entered the world.
    Don't let this woman castrate you!
    My papa is a night zombie, a dorlis.
    Shave all these sinful women!
    A man without a face who possesses women while they sleep. . .
    Men produce, women reproduce.
    Every night papa plants his seeds in women and every year he reaps a heap of kids.
    "In zoology, the dominant male is the individual in the group of animals. . .".
    You are a son without a crown or a heritage.
    ". . . that the other members follow whom they obey and to whom they submit".
    a hen doesn't sing before a rooster!
    My papa is a nightmare.
    I don't need a man.
    Toughen your nuts, faggot!
    Stone these disobedient women!
    You don't need a papa.
    show her which of you pisses further.
    And he doesn't need you.
    be man, dammit !
    My papa is a king.
    The Bible said it: "Man wasn't created because of woman, but woman was created
    because of man".
    The king of the carnival puppets.
    fagot! Fagot! Fagot!
    Circumcise these shameless women!
    how can you allow a woman to give you orders?
    My mama is a witch.
    A woman who seduces is a she-devil.
    And my papa she devoured.

After a long struggle, the man manages to tear off his mask.
Long silence.

VOICE: A dark night, in the small hours of his life, a *bwabwa* puppet man slips falls over and comes to grief in a puddle of syrup and finds himself standing upside down, covered by a rainbow. And it is with great sadness filled with joy that the Vaval man, the carnival king, discovers he is dead.

Dead. He's dead.
Object-man. Man of women-without a mother without-a father-without children. Dead.
Lost man. The blind man without a heart or a face. Dead.
Conquest man. Liar man rooster dog vermin man. Dead.

He is survived by a dancing procession of tearful dolls with abandoned boobs, a string of children without papas, bastard children born by waving a tragic rod, an avalanche of feathers, stray bullets, sweet-talking words, and many a destroyed pubis.

After his brutal disappearance, an infinite silence roars within him. And for the first time since the flesh of an eternity, he feels the slow hatching of the *doum-doum* of his heart.

Ladies and gentlemen, society, congregation, company, at this nostalgic hour when the night coils in the hollow of the early morning, once upon a time, twice, three times, an infinity of times upon a time, a man stood next to his dead body.

Djablès lights a big fire.
The man throws his mask in it.

WOMAN: (*Singing*)
Anmwé manman lalinn-o
Manman bèlté lannuit
wouvè lapòt syèl-la, é

Anmwé manman lalinn-o
Tout zétwèl klendendé
fè syèl-la pétayé, nou mélé!

Anmwé manman lalinn-o
Kléré tout ti pasaj
tout ti tras nou pilé
wouvè chimen pasaj
pou nou sa travèsé

Anmwè, man kriyé anmwé-o
chimen lapòt pasaj
wouvè lapòt chimen
kwazé lé sèt pasaj
dékwazé kat chimen

Anmwé, man kriyé anmwé-o
Ki anlè ki anba
ki douvan ki dèyè
andidan andèwò
pasi pala lòtbò

Anmwé, sé anmwé man ka kriyé
sa ki anba monté
sa ki anlè désann
sa ki étenn kléré
kléré sa ki annwè

Anmwé, sé anmwé man ka chanté
lapli bèkté latè
latè tijé dan syèl
tout sikré ki séré
éklò an gran limyè

Aham-bo-ibo, Aham-bo-ibo,
Aham-bo-ibo, Aham-bo-ibo

Andèwò ka vèglé-w, fèmé lapo dé zyé-w,
annwèsè a fon kè-w, an limyè ka séré,
Fo-w sa touvé solèy, séré an fon lannuit,
Ni sa ou ka gadé, san jen wè lavérité, nou mélé!

Aham-bo-ibo, Aham-bo-ibo,
Aham-bo-ibo, Aham-bo-ibo

Ni sa-w konprann ou wè,
Sé pa sa pou ou kwè,
Ni sa-w kouté pou tann,
san pa janmen konprann,
Ni sa-w konprann ou ni,
ka mété-w toutouni,
Ni sa ou ka valé, mi lang-ou za ka brilé-w, nou mélé!

Wooo! Nou mélé!

Kwazé dékwazé lékat
Dékwazé kwazé léwuit
tèt anwo ka tètanba
wopa dékwazé lépa
kochi dékochi chimen
kabouya démélé mwen
anchouké sa ki anlè
flè fléché anfon latè
Woy!
Wouvè fenmen
wouvè épi fenmen
sa ki fenmen wouvè
sa ki doubout tonbé
sa ki étenn kléré

Limyè limen
Limyè kléré chimen
dépayé tout chimen chyen
wondi déwondi lékat chimen
èk dékalé twa senk,
sèt bèl solèy lannuit. . .

Translation:

Mother-Moon, O
Night Beauty
Open the door of the sky for us

Mother-Moon, O
Who makes all the stars sparkle
and the sky blaze

Mother-Moon, O
Illuminate all passages
All paths visited
Clear the way for our passage
Allow us to cross

O, in your direction I cry
Path portal of passages
Clear the way of the paths
Uncross the four paths

May my cry echo
On high and on low
In front and behind
Here, there, elsewhere

Yes, may my cry echo
And may what lies below appear
What is above disappear
What is dark lighten
Shed light on what lies in the shadows

O, may my cry echo
the rain peck at the dirt
the earth reach up toward the sky
all the buried secrets
hatch in the light of day

Aham-bo-ibo, Aham-bo-ibo,
Aham-bo-ibo, Aham-bo-ibo

Appearances fool you,
close the portal of your eyes
In the darkness of your heart
hides a light,
Learn to find the sun
hidden in the night,
-What you don't see
in reality therein lies!

Aham-bo-ibo, Aham-bo-ibo,
Aham-bo-ibo, Aham-bo-ibo

What you believe you see,
isn't what you should believe,
What you hear,
you don't how to comprehend,
What you think you possess,
in truth disposes you
What it is you swallow
sets your tongue on fire!

Woah we are entangled
Cross and uncross the four
Cross and uncross the eight
What is standing up will be upside down
woah uncross the steps
fold and unfold the paths
untangle the knots
anchor what floats
may the flour grow in the bosom of the earth

Open close
open and close
what is closed may open
what has fallen may get up
what is extinguished burns again

Light turn on
Illuminate the path
Uncover the lost trail
Encircle and unloop the four paths,
and dissect three, five,
seven beautiful night suns

Three long conch shell calls. Three paths clear.

White

The pale sky counts the stars.
The man and the woman are wearing white.

MAN: Djablès, Queen Djablès. You are not a witch, but rather a magician. Your lips have made me be born again.

WOMAN: All you did was to embrace your courage.

MAN: The little rooster is dead.

WOMAN: And now it is daybreak.

MAN: My path has opened up. I can retrace my steps.

WOMAN: Go now, and travel beyond the horizon.

The MAN makes his way along a path. Then he retraces his steps.

MAN: And... you?

WOMAN: Me?

MAN: Are you staying here?

WOMAN: My kingdom is here.

MAN: And me, I go back to my cinder block shack?

WOMAN: You are free.

Silence.

MAN: So... this is goodbye?

WOMAN: Yes. Unless you're dreaming of another tête à tête with Ladjablès?

MAN: Goodbye, then.

The man leaves for a while. Returns again.

MAN: But I am no longer afraid. I no longer have a reason to flee.

WOMAN: That's because you have found the final key for your passage.

The fourth path lights up. The man sits down, contemplates it.

MAN: Tell me why, Queen Djablès, why a woman as beautiful as you has to drag along such an ugly leg? It's true that your hoof must be ashamed to limp next to such a pretty foot, and your pretty foot must be so angry to live with such an unsightly hoof.

WOMAN: I'm a perfectly imperfect woman.

MAN: I see that, but do you like to walk with an uneven gate like that?

WOMAN: Before, when the devil was a little boy, before, I lived among others. I lived among those men and women who walked proudly and follow in the footsteps of those who preceded them on the long journey. I walked alongside them for a long time on the well-traveled trails day after day, sun after sun, moon after moon, roaming across the belly of the earth's paths, circuits, journeys. I lived among those whose feet take root in the belly of the earth in order to erect their totems and cathedrals. On one still sleepy morning when the sun struggled to emerge from the clouds, I distanced myself. I distanced myself from this millenary path only to land in a wild place. This piece of warm dirt felt like an escape rather than a conquest, more like an escape to an unknown side of the world. So I began to dance. Dance freely. Like a drunken butterfly among the wildflowers. I danced for this infinite land. But the others saw me. They cried out my name to warn me of danger. Shouted out against my audacious escape. Ordered me to retrace my steps back to the right path, the one carved out eons ago by those who came before them. But I kept dancing. I was becoming so beautiful so light so luminous. They protested against my rebellion and cursed my strange dance in vain, I rode the perfumed wave of this wild land to the brilliant blue of the sky. They screamed blasphemies, called me a witch, shaped their bitter insults into a ball that they hurled at me. I was supposed to cease my indecent dance and conform my steps to the appropriate binary rhythm. Then they put a curse on me. To hinder the wild steps of my dance. A hoof. Heavy. To weigh me to the ground, to make me heavy, and to forbid me from walking proudly among others. They tripped me up. But my dance is unstoppable. This hoof is the wild part of me. Formidable wildness for a people who follow the well-traveled paths. My foot and my hoof make me what I am. A woman. Wild. A wild woman.

MAN: Wild woman. I'm not familiar with this breed of women.

WOMAN: I'm the daughter of an eclipse. Two unreachable worlds coexist within me. Night and day. The visible and the invisible. I live at the edge of the twilight. In order to find me you must know how to walk the tightrope on the hinge of time.

MAN: We had a date. Under an unreal sky at the crossroads of these terrifying trails.

WOMAN: Now you see more clearly. One by one, the stars are fading. It's time to leave, Syrup Man.

MAN: Man. Call me Man.

Silence.

WOMAN: Goodbye then, Man.

MAN. Goodbye.

He leaves, and then comes back.

MAN: But you spared me. You didn't devour me or rip out my brain. Even though I'm a monster with women. You have every reason to seek revenge.

WOMAN: I'm not in looking for revenge against men, I'm just trying to change their course. Force them to abandon their sacred totems, tear away their narrow exterior, hide out in their undergrowth to teach them nakedness and silence. So that they may come to desire themselves in the wild pulsing beneath their skin.

The man weeps.

MAN: Queen Djablès, I want you. It's like a sacred fire burning inside me. I have never desired anyone this much. This fire, I have never felt it. My heart has changed. I'm no longer afraid of you.

The woman takes his face in her hands and kisses his tears.

WOMAN: Then don't call me Djablès anymore. Call me Woman.

MAN: Woman?. . . You aren't the woman I was looking for, you're the one I found.

WOMAN: Wild women are more common than you think.

MAN: But you're not like other women.

WOMAN: And you aren't like other men.

MAN: So tell me how to love you.

WOMAN: Love yourself as you are. Love me as I am.
    Let's not upstage each other.
    Let's explore both our territories without colonizing each other.
    Let's walk, our bodies side by side, without cannibalizing each other.

Their bodies fuse. Darkness.

Epilogue

The morning after carnival under the blue eye of the sky. Washed up on a sidewalk of the city, a man lies asleep.
A car zooms past, the man wakes up with a start, with some difficulty, stands up, looks up and down the deserted street. He seems disoriented.

MAN: And when just before daybreak the Gray Kingbird sings *piripiri*,
    when you part the curtains of your numbed eyelids,
    I, your incubus, your night zombie, your *dorlis*
    I, the vagabond will have long since taken leave.

    You will have left without a gesture, without a caress.
    Evaporated without so much as leaving an address,
    not without having reanimated my once distraught heart
    within which now courses my regenerated sap.

    Djablès. . .

Darkness.

STREET SAD
by
Luc Saint-Éloy

GUADELOUPE

translation by Josh Cohen

Characters:

HER
> Young prostitute. No attachments to the world left. Nothing scares her. She sells herself when she feels like it; it's a game. A taste for mischief sends her into the night like an enemy penetrating conquerable lands, and she spits words like cannonballs. She is what she is and nothing can change that.
>
> Age: between 25 and 30 years old.

HIM
> Psycho? Voyeur? Killer?
> The tree hiding the forest.
>
> Age: between 30 and 40 years old.

Night. A woman sits on a bench; nobody is around. She stares at the ground. She talks to herself, hums.

A man approaches. He stops in the dark to better watch her.

A few moments later:

THE MAN: Hey! Girl! The one talking to yourself. . . . I've been watching you. Sitting there. It's like you're waiting for something to happen. But this place is empty. People only come here when there's a concert. . . . It's not right to be alone here, like this, just sitting there in the same spot, in the same place, waiting. Especially if you're a woman—like you.

I've been watching you.

THE GIRL: Like a hunter spotting his prey. Or a peeping Tom. But you haven't made a move. What're you waiting for? Why don't you just move on?

Where I'm from, in my country, we call what you're doing, "*Faire le mako.*"

And what I'm doing here, right now. What I'll be doing in five minutes, is exactly nobody's business but mine. If you're looking for a little company, I recommend heading on over to La Rue Budapest.

THE MAN: If I were you, I wouldn't be acting so high and mighty around other people like that.

THE GIRL: Ha. Funny, trying to scare me hiding in the dark like that like a monster. I knew you were there; I knew you'd been following me—you followed me all the way here drooling like an idiot, and you had no idea that I knew I was being followed.

THE MAN: Wait—who was following you? I was just going wherever my steps took me.

THE GIRL: Oh, and your steps just happened to take you wherever mine took me, just like that. When we were behind the train station earlier, when I made those two loops around the newspaper stand, I could have hid up against the wall and then unloaded my pepper spray right in your face, you know.

THE MAN: Easy. My steps took me where your steps took you: it just happened.

THE GIRL: Fine. Whaddaya want? What's your vibe? What're you into?

THE MAN: You have nothing to fear. I don't want to hurt you.

THE GIRL: (*Laughing*) Don't worry, man. I'm not your scared type. Long as I've been out here, alone, at night, it's been clear to me that horny dudes are far more scared than the girls they're creeping on. Even on Saturday nights when they all come out after their depressing little workweeks with their ugly faces: they don't scare me. You've got the wrong prey, man.

THE MAN: Being so sure of yourself might throw your game off. What are those things called, you know. . . ice pops. People used to get ice pops stuffed in their asses: that shut them up.

THE GIRL: Ohhh. So, you followed me all the way here just to sell me *ice pops*? Might want a new profession, pal, if you're trying to work nights. A good businessman operates *transparently*. Only rapists and killers hide themselves like you're doing—like a coward.

Silence.

What're you waiting for?

Silence.

I can't hear you—what'd you say?

Silence.

You want me to come into the dark so I can get raped?

Silence.

Is that what you want?

THE MAN: It's the sound of the waves that keep the little fish from sleeping—

THE GIRL: What?

THE MAN: I said: it's the sound of the waves that keep the little fish from sleeping—

THE GIRL: Right. After ice pops: fish. Of course. And then it'll be boars, chickens, Barilla's linguine, the galaxies, the moon, the stars, the sun, the universe—what do you want? What're you into?

THE MAN: I said, I don't want to hurt you.

THE GIRL: So then what's your problem?

THE MAN: You're too sweet, when you flirt.

THE GIRL: You been with me?

THE MAN: I just *know* you, that's all.

THE GIRL: Oh, and I did some stuff you liked—got it. You want a lil more then? Don't be mean, come on: come out. I choose my clients on their faces. I've got what you want, man, I'm the one who's got you all hot and bothered in the shadows, and you know it. Don't act like you know me. I know your kind: creeps. You, for example, let's see, you, you spend your days set up right in the middle of the sidewalk dying to get a little look, you set your sights on anything that moves, your mouth open, you drool, you just want a taste, stilettos kill you, a little ass, legs, thighs, a tight mini-skirt. The brain, the heart, whatever's going on on the inside—you couldn't care less. It's from behind that you decide who's worth it, right? That's what gets you hard. Obvious son of a bitch. It's not women that obsess you—it's their asses. Their perfect little asses. And that gets under your skin, it burns, it itches—and, so, you need it, now. A look is not enough. You're hungry. You're thirsty.

Our desires want to be realities. The beast in us wakes up ready to do whatever, however, no matter what the cost—and then, voila, the solution, it was there all along: whores! Perfect. Whores. Drop a few bills and: paradise.

But I wonder: tell me: if we weren't here, in this world, us whores, what would happen to you? What would you look like if we weren't here to heal you and your mob of lunatics?

No—god bless whores. God bless the streets where whores run. Amen.

THE MAN: (*A little nervous*) Don't be so naïve. Nobody ever comes here. I could attack you, I could rape you, I could make you feel the worst things possible—I could make you shut up so I didn't have to listen to your dirty shit.

THE GIRL: Oh, don't hold back, sweetie. Come show the nice little lady what you got. Come on. . . What, you getting bored of my kind of whore? I know, you want me to run—you want me *to run* into the dark so you can pounce on me. Come on, sweetie. We'll see how long you last staying like that in the shadows. I'll make you wish you'd never creeped on me.

THE MAN: I said, I don't want to hurt you.

THE GIRL: I know what you want. I know your kind. Look. This time of night, there're hundreds of guys like you, huddled on street corners waiting for hours like total losers. I see them every day. The biggest cowards stay in the dark waiting forever and then they just end up leaving. But the others, the ones who can't stop staring, the ones on fire with their needs, whose faces tell you everything their tiny little brains can't keep in—we throw them a bone, and they follow: they crawl after us.

THE MAN: Like flies. They circle you. And then when you pick them up they stick to you like shit.

THE GIRL: (*Proud*) And they pay, yes, sir, they pay to eat shit. They pay. They leave their little stations, and they come to us, like their wives and mothers go shopping. And we are the sellers of pleasure. We sell it to them, and they eat it up like animals, their stomachs huge, and they drool: like pigs. Poor fools. I hate all my clients. So, indeed, they pay. Yes, sir. But if they only knew what was simmering in my sacred whore's body, I swear, they'd jet faster than a rocket.

Long pause.

What you don't realize, all of you, is that my flesh isn't only a promised land. It's not sex you want. It's my entire body you poison, it's my soul, the world you hollow out, and it's your grandmother, your mother, your little sister, your daughter, who watch you, and whose insides explode with every thrust into my belly.

THE MAN: You're off your rocker, girl. . .

THE GIRL: Damn you all! I'll put a curse on you in the name of all women, in the name of my body, in the name of our ruined bodies, in the name of my broken life—May you be damned! . . .

A long silence. The man slowly emerges from the shadows.

I know what you're thinking, hiding out in the darkness of your cowardly silence. You're all the same. Just a mob of lunatics. I'm never moving from here. You're the foreigner.

The man approaches, quietly, and freezes behind her back. He speaks suddenly in a serious voice:

THE MAN: What foreigner?

She jumps, turns around. They're face to face; they stare at each other.

She suddenly gets furious, and sets off fuming.

THE MAN: (*Crying out, quickly*) You're leaving because we are the same.

She stops short. Looks at him warily.

THE GIRL: White, black, red, yellow, green—I don't give a shit! A lunatic, a psycho who'd jump all over me, who'd rape me, who'd cut my throat, who'd send me dancing into the next world—yeah. That's what I wanted instead of . . .

THE MAN: (*Yelling*) Stop!

THE GIRL: Fine. . . . Got cash? Trying to fuck?

Silence.

Answer me. Got cash?

THE MAN: I don't want your body, or sex.

THE GIRL: Fine. What do you want me to be then? Your mother? Your priest? Same price either way. Same animal, same skin. . .

THE MAN: Does it have to be all about hard cash and sex between us?

THE GIRL: What—you want me to waste my time?

He holds out a bill.

THE MAN: I followed you because I wanted to understand you—to listen to you, to talk to you.

She looks at him.

THE GIRL: I don't like that look. You smile but your eyes don't.

THE MAN: Old habit. Being black taught me to smile with just my lips.

THE GIRL: You wanna write your life story then?

THE MAN: I want to be with you—to understand you.

She takes the bill he has been holding out.

THE GIRL: You look at me and you ask yourself, Why? Why. Why not, baby? I'm a whore and so what. I am what I am. Don't worry, I wasn't born a whore. No woman is. You become one. And I am one, a real one. My ass is a golden ticket to a future with the Devil, because I didn't obey the rules of little baby Jesus.

Is it my fault if I was born black in a country whose air stinks of no future, where men think only of sex, and women rent it out for a plate of red beans and pigtail? Is it my fault if I—the fruit of a plate of red beans and pigtail—if I had to leave my heaven motherless and fatherless, with my guts full of nothing?

"You stink of misery, young lady. You're black, you have no degree, you're not even pretty. Your mother played a cruel trick, bringing you into this world. If you were a man I'd tell you to take refuge in the army—that's where your kind belongs. But you're nothing but a woman: a poor, black woman. Try to live. Death will drag you out of this hornet's nest of life."

What am I supposed to do to fight that? I know! Become a whore! It's better than the army. You keep your freedom. And if you're good at it, you might even get a little respect. So, voilà: whore. But a good whore, better than a shitty nurse, or a postal worker. I'm not proud, but I am not ashamed, either. I own the shittiness of my existence. I'm the kind of creature who could have something buzzing all over her skin, and it won't matter whether they're the kind of flies that eat shit, or honeybees, or blowflies, or whatever.

Insult, injury, that's my daily bread. And I deal with it, because it's my job.

THE MAN: These days, misery is to man what the earth is to plants. It flowers everywhere—and we really deserve it. The one sole path that leads to total nothingness: we've discovered it. But you, you are not like the others. . . . No, you are not like the others. . . . I knew it the first time.

THE GIRL: What first time?

THE MAN: The first time. . .

THE GIRL: What first time?

THE MAN: Do you know the story of that umbrella? I could tell you—step for step—how it ended up in your possession: it was about a week ago, bad weather, on the corner of Boulevard Voltaire. You were the only one outside who didn't run when it started raining. A man planted himself right in front of you; he looked at you. Here, take it. . . Absent minded. . . all crumpled up. You watched. The tears and the rain cut you off from the world. He put it in your hand. But you couldn't see anything—

I disappeared.

THE GIRL: It was you—

THE MAN: It was me. The very first time. There, that night, and then tonight, I saw you again—I didn't know I followed you.

She gives him back the umbrella, almost stupefied.

THE GIRL: Here—thanks, thanks. . .

THE MAN: No—keep it. It's a gift. The other day: the tears, under the rain. . . the other day. . .

THE GIRL: That's how it is. . . Now that he's gone. . . his absence. . . and they flow. . . and I see him. . . I see him again. . . that's how it is. . .

THE MAN: Is it possible to love so much then. . . spending nights. . .

THE GIRL: I loved him and he loved me. Like children: simply. We loved each other simply.

THE MAN: He pushed you to move in. Proof—of love?

She traces the outline of a corpse on the ground.

THE GIRL: There. Murdered like a dog. I swore I'd never come back. A year later: all forgotten, nothing learned. Memory is like television. We watch our lives pass on screens. We die, we're born: twenty times; a hundred times; a thousand times. Everyone we love, and everyone we hate, passes by.

THE MAN: Who. . . is—?

THE GIRL: My life. Jeannot. My own flesh and blood. One never forgets. After I was born my poor, single mother gave birth to my little brother Jeannot.

Who was the father? Nobody knew. He was dropped into the world like a perfect little turd. Fifteen days later, without even looking at him, my mother took him to Manzelle Adele and she forgot him for eight years—and then—when he came home—it was the most beautiful day of my life.

THE MAN: (*Offering a cigarette*) Here—

THE GIRL: My mother never accepted him. For years he had to endure the stupidest, the meanest, punishments.

She gets angry.

Mr. Leopold, the director of the school, with his perfect monkey's suit-and-tie, comes and knocks at our door one dat, it was a Tuesday, noon. He accused Jeannot of scraping the hood of his Model 204 Peugeot. "A Peugeot! 204! Entirely new. Madame, do you understand? His friends saw it, they'd testify. This kid needs to learn to respect other people's property. Respecting other people's property is as essential as respecting oneself. If you want to build responsible and respectable men, you have to act now, you must be vigilant. . . Oh! Oh! Can you imagine. . . a Peugeot 204. . . Brand new. Bring little Jeannot here right now."

Momma takes a step back. Then she looks daggers at the man in the monkey suit and screams, "Get out! Get out of my house! There are no gangsters in this house."

She slams the door, and then, like a cyclone, without any explanation, she beats Jeannot worse than a mother had ever beaten her son. She hit him for hours, unleashing all of the hate that had stored up in her abandoned heart. When she'd had enough, she collapsed on the couch like a fat, exhausted cow, in a pool of cotton balls.

Jeannot lay in the corner of his room like a dirty pile of laundry.

I took a good ten minutes to gather him close to me, a bit like a hen gathering her chicks. I held him to my chest with all my force. A storm raged inside of him, his little face changed. I didn't want his heart to explode. I held him tighter, as tight as I could, so that he'd become calm like water. My brother was 12. It was the first time I'd seen him cry.

Pain was born in our red eyes, with the help of some kind of potion, some magic. Strange feeling swirled about, uniting us. New things happened to us, without warning, and they were scarily good. On his trembling lips, I gently placed mine, dreamlike. Once, twice, again, endlessly, soft little kisses, and they were warm. We stayed like that, curled up, our bodies and souls intertwined, protecting each other, into the night. Our hearts spoke to each other. Love, to love, to be loved—to love each other. To become one with another, one heart full of love, joy. . . and hate.

We'd stick together forever, I'd be the shirt on his back.

When he yelled, "TIMBER!", I'd yell, "CHOP IT ALL DOWN!"

She smiles; sees the man again.

THE MAN: (*Playing along*) He'd say, "TIMBER!"—

THE GIRL: (*Overcome with joy, electrified*) CHOP IT ALL DOWN!
When we came here, we lived in a dirty small room, in Barbès. That's where he made up our favorite game:
She laughs
"And so what do we do when we get bored in Paris?!"
I'd answer:
"We remember. . . "
She laughs
We laughed like crazy.
Her memories flood back. She acts them out.
"And in Paris, what do we do when get bored?"
"We remember"
She bursts out in laughter.
"Robe à dentelles, ki douvan mwen, robe à dentelles ka brennen byen, gadé dantèl ki douvan mwen."
It was Mama Fify, Papa Jacoby's neighbor. She always had so many stories.
She smiles. At the end of her story, she stops, almost suddenly, with a touch of jealousy.

When Miss Geraldine Dingwall gets off the boat, it's America. He was crazy about it. . .

THE MAN: (*Jumps up*) Which America? The one where we used to meet up, everybody packing, on the corner of 12th avenue?

THE GIRL: No. The one Jeannot was talking about.

THE MAN: But which? The one that makes the whole world shake? Or the real America, the America of the death penalty, who wastes a little boy in an electric chair. . .

THE GIRL: No. The America of Angela Davis. Of great black leaders. Of Geraldine Dingwall, who sang Big Country—Jeannot loved her like crazy. She taught him about New York. "It's the biggest city in the biggest country in the world! Do you know what happens in New York?"

He used to say that nonstop. And blah blah blah—music, blues, jazz.

"This one really gets me, listen. This is Billie Holliday. And this is Aretha Franklin. And this is Armstrong."

Offstage we hear bits and pieces of jazz.

Lionel Hampton, Bessie Smith, Count Basie, Mahalia Jackson. . . the music spoke to him in all kinds of ways. That Geraldine Dingwall totally changed him.

When they left each other, from one dat to the next, he renamed himself Jonathan, now a black American citizen. [In English]: "Ok, sister. My name is Jonathan, Jonathan Jackson."

Our little dirty maid's room in Barbès became America in no time at all.

All four walls were covered with the American greats: Martin Luther King, Angela Davis, Marcus Garvey, Malcolm X. . . all the great black Americans. . .

She looks off.

"But Jeannot. . . "
"Hey! I'm Jonathan, ok—you know."
"Ok, ok, d'accord, brother, you are, no, oui, ok, your name is Jonathan. . . um. . . hey! Brother!"

She looks at the walls.

"Is there really no space for the others? You know. . . Ignace, Delgrès, Toussaint Louverture, Frantz Fanon."

She chews gum.

Bubble gum—he always had bubble gum, American bubble gum, in his mouth, and he'd look at me with his American face and he'd say:

"Yes, sister, yeah. One day we'll move. Ok. They'll all be there, ok, darling, everybody will be there. . . Ok." And he'd hug me. He was like that. We always loved each other. He wanted me to call him Jonathan, so I called him Jonathan. He wanted me to like his music, so I liked black American music. I like it.

She approaches the outline of the corpse on the ground.

> That day. . . Saturday. . . 6 pm. . .
> He left the house with a smile, his American jacket on his back.
> "Ciao, darling, the concert's at 8."
> "Ciao, Jonathan, ciao."
> It was the last time I saw him. They took him from me. Murdered like a dog.
> Not a day goes by when I don't see his murder happening before my eyes, like images in a tabloid.
> Not a day goes by when I don't think about that shit Saturday. I've dreamt so many times of a giant drop of blood drowning the two of us—I should have gone with him, should have protected him from the vermin, from the knife of that filthy, huge pig, with his dirty face, that stupid thug, diseased monster.
> Security, they said! Security! Jeannot was protected by security *assassins*. Murderers.
> I've imagined it so often: panicked, stuck, deep in the crowd, *hot*, that filthy pig's blade shining in the sun: the crowd ran, and screamed, in all directions. . . .
> "Murdered!"
> Yes, but don't worry, dear sir, it's just a black guy, it's no big deal, nothing to be sad about.
> If he'd stayed under the coconut trees, he'd still be alive.
> "There were so many of them," "they looked threatening," said the other asshole, defending himself, making excuses for killing my Jeannot. And the cops believed him: accomplices. All of them: assholes.
> "Music drives black people crazy. It makes them dangerous, it makes them want to get the White Man. Every time there's a concert in this place, we double our security, yes, indeed, Mr. Journalist. Check your sources before you cry racism!"
> Dirty rotten liars. Dead for nothing, Jeannot. My Jeannot. Just like that. Because he lived in a country where the color of his skin sets maniacs off like bulls seeing red. . . . If only I had been there.

THE MAN: Yesterday I saw a boy pretending to kill his friend. Children imitate adults. They don't know that adults aren't children. Killing isn't child's play.

She takes a sheet of paper from between her breasts and hands it to him.

THE GIRL: Here.

Offstage, we hear a man reading the paper.

> "The painter has his brushes,
> The poet, his pen,
> The wind, its birds,
> The sea, her waves
> The iguana's hot,
> The bear is cold"
>
> Nicolas Guillén

She takes the paper back.

THE GIRL: And me, I had Jeannot, Jonathan. . .

Silence.

THE MAN: Life's written on paper, but death is rock-solid. What good are memories for if mourning is so useless?

You speak, now, of then; yesterday, tomorrow, today, a year ago. You cling to time with words only you understand. But everything you say, everything you do—it's for nothing.

Living, dying, pleasure, pain: it's all the same. The end always comes.

You rush to get the train at 7:30, on the dot, and at 7:30 all the zombies watch you rushing to get in past the doors right before they close, and then you get in, and when you do, they make a little space for you.

And you take your place, there, on the orange bench, just fitting in, plopping down onto an ass drawn in black ink.

And there you sit: two idiots inevitably watching you, a little old lady doing the crossword, all three of whom had shuffled about in sync to make a place for you, and now they stare at you.

Why?

All the wise men in the world, all the shrinks, all the philosophers, everybody who knows the why of things: they'll give you a why, a real why, they'll tell you how sitting in that exact spot affects everybody but you. That ass drawn in black ink on the orange bench: everything you always wanted to know, but never dared asking, they'll tell you why you sit down right on it.

I'll tell you something more simple: it's evidence. There was no grand conspiracy to make a place for you at 7:30 on the dot on this train car. You saw it—the ass drawn in ink—when you sat down. Nobody wanted the seat because everybody knew perfectly well that if they did they'd walk around with the ass of the moron who'd sat on that seat stuck to their backside all day, and you, but you, you, of course, you happily sat right down.

No accident there.

Because of everybody on that train you were the only one willing to put your ass on the ass of a stranger. Other people were disturbed by the thought, but you, that's your job; it wasn't an accident: you chose it. You sat because you wanted to. You were game.

It's like dying. It disturbs others. But you, you'll die when you're ready, because it's time. People always think it's unjust to die in an accident, but one never dies by pure chance: it's your return ticket.

We can't go backwards. So what's the point of going back and forth, of dwelling in the past, of even thinking about it, when the task is to move on? It's by walking straight, not looking back, that I stumbled upon you tonight: I followed you without knowing why, I understood nothing, because you were the one leading—you wanted me to follow you, to find you. Your steps led mine here.

And that's why there's nobody else here, now, at this time of night, because nobody, not a cat, not even an insect, nobody dares approach us. We're alone.

Soon we'll have to come to blows, as if that were the only way out, the only way to come together.

All around, the rest of the animals are hidden in their corners of this monstrous city; they know we're not their kind. It's the law. The world has always been a jungle. Cities are full of savage beasts tossed into the streets, one after the other, according to a law we will never, ever, grasp.

Oh. Oh, oh, oh. It's too late. Don't you get it? Killing is natural. Like sleeping, eating, talking, resting, drinking. Have to live with the times

THE GIRL: My time is Jeannot's. I don't give a shit about the rest.

THE MAN: No! No, the rest is you, is me. Look at us. You were talking just now like somebody who knew the language of war, of the jungle, of all the furious beasts who want nothing more than to bash, to kill. It's me you wanted to crush underfoot. . . . because it's winter everywhere in your body.

And the truth is, we can't resist long when we're alone in the storm. You're nothing more than a little ball of drifting youth with nobody to talk to and just dying for it. Pain is like that. It makes us alone. People all around you, but you're alone. All night, in every neighborhood of Paris, alone. The city is pitiless. It's nothing but pedophiles and whores. . . the rest are lost souls. . . nobody to talk to you when you need to talk. . . I wander the night. . . pedophiles, whores, lost souls.

You enter the first dive bar you see: it doesn't matter which. You stay at the bar an hour, two hours, three hours, you look for somebody who looks like you, you look for somebody who might want to talk to you. Nobody's like you. Some howl with laughter; others drool, eyelids fluttering; two people, there, in the corner, love each other like famished beasts; a woman in the corner smokes a joint going on about her miserable boyfriend.

You gain ground, you gain back your territory, you go round and around, like a crab at the bottom of a bucket, and you stumble across them: the whores, the pedophiles, the lost souls. Like the country bumpkin says, "It's too much." Exactly. It's too much. So many, too many, of my little sisters on the street, they cheat, they act proud, arrogant; they rebel. But there's absolutely nothing in their dirty little heads. Last week two of them—two little idiots—I screwed them, finished in less than a minute. That's it! All done.

THE GIRL: I want to put my head on his shoulder. So gently.

THE MAN: You're nothing when you have nothing left. We treat you like dirt; you become an animal.

THE GIRL: I don't want to think anymore.

THE MAN: As a thing, you're nothing more than a pile of dirty laundry. As an animal, you're worse than the beast who has no other choice but to hunt in order to exist.

I chose to be the beast that kills, free of feelings, shamed neither by God nor men.

THE GIRL: I think of the good times. That helps me to deal with the world's evils.

THE MAN: Your words thundered in the night like bullets.

THE GIRL: I didn't want to come back.

THE MAN: I didn't know people like you existed.

THE GIRL: To leave.

THE MAN: You'll leave here.

THE GIRL: I've talked a lot. I've said too much about it, haven't I?

THE MAN: Some people hide their pain like a dirty little sickness. You, your sadness, you parade it down the street like you were walking a dog on a leash.

You need to go now.

THE GIRL: I said too much. This night isn't like other nights. . . . Here, take your money—

She holds out the bill.

THE MAN: No, keep it.

THE GIRL: My pain belongs to me. You didn't pay for that.

THE MAN: (*Nervous*) It's me—I'm the one who was talking. Keep it.

She plays the whore. Touches him.

THE MAN: What are you doing. . .

THE GIRL: You'll get your money's worth, baby. . .

THE MAN: (*Stepping back*) I don't want your body.

THE GIRL: Take me. And if you want, we can keep on talking, too.

She grabs him.

THE MAN: Let me go.

THE GIRL: (*She looks him up and down.*) I was nasty to you, so? You're dying for it, and that kills you. Forget what I said.

THE MAN: You must go.

THE GIRL: I can tell: you're dying of desire. (*She laughs.*)

THE MAN: Enough! You don't know anything.

THE GIRL: So what do you know that I don't?

THE MAN: Time is going to cease because you don't get it. We can't see time passing: that's how it is. It's like staring into a bottomless hole. An endless empty chain of emptiness. Longer than an endless tunnel. Where it's headed, where it started, where it ends: you understand nothing. Every question leads to another question, every question gets swallowed up by the tunnel. A ladder: it's a huge, long ladder.

It's a mirror with no reflection. Nowhere, nothing.

Nothing. But there are those who dance, and those who play. You dance, because the game isn't the game you want to play. But who—who is willing to pull the strings?

Too many whys. Too much asking. You need to leave this place—go.

THE GIRL: You talk like an unreadable book.

THE MAN: I talk like one who is what he is, and knows what he is. And if I say, You need to leave, you need to leave.

THE GIRL: I do what I want. I stopped taking orders a long time ago.

THE MAN: I'd have been long gone if I were you. Look at my hands.

THE GIRL: What about them?

THE MAN: These hands kill. I'm the killer of girls the police are looking for. I strangled them with these hands to calm myself: to stop my suffering, to bury my impotent shame. I crush their heads. I feet them die in my hands. The harder they fight back, the greater the pleasure I feel, a pleasure mixed with power, stronger than anything sexual. That feeling gets me, hard. It's my drug. And these hands, they get it for me when I need it.

Understand now?

THE GIRL: (*Bursting out in laughter*) Hahahah!

THE MAN: Go.

THE GIRL: (*Laughing*) A real, live killer. With hands that strangle. How about a bullfighter, too? Come on. I'll be the bull, the big, fat cow: I'll charge. Come on. We're in the arena, and you're trying to kill me. For the fun of it.

Come on, baby. I'll charge.

She sings:

Toreador! Prends gaaarddee!

A dance between bull and bullfighter starts.

THE MAN: Don't be an idiot.

THE GIRL: TOREADOR! Take me. Come on.

THE MAN: Go.

THE GIRL: Preenddss gaarddee!

THE MAN: Crazt girl!!

THE GIRL: Ole, ole! Come on, baby.

THE MAN: Last week, two of them—

THE GIRL: Let's go! Take me.

THE MAN: Smashed to pieces. These two little beasts.

THE GIRL: Ole! Let's go, baby.

THE MAN: I'm telling you: in two minutes, this is all over.

They turn circles; the dance speeds up.

THE GIRL: It's not over, baby! Ole!

THE MAN: You must have exhausted even your whore of a mother.

THE GIRL: Think about your mother, baby. Come on now. . .

THE MAN: That bitch trying to sink her hooks into me. Trying to mother me as if I were her disgusting little son—let's go. It's over.

THE GIRL: Voilà, the problem. And you're right, baby. You're right. Your mother was very much a woman. . . carry on.

THE MAN: They're all nasty bitches, I said. They all need a good beating.

THE GIRL: They annoy you, baby. Get under your skin.

THE MAN: They trap the first idiot that comes their way, and then they take vengeance on their sons.

THE GIRL: Take vengeance, baby! Take me if, if that's what does it for you.

THE MAN: They're all monsters.

THE GIRL: Poor baby.

THE MAN: Two minutes: then it's over.

THE GIRL: Right, okay, let's go, baby. Ole. . . ole. . . it's not over yet.

He shoves the page of a newspaper in front of her face like a shield. She stops cold, tears the newspaper from his hands. After a few seconds, she reads.

> "THE RED-LIGHT KILLER HAS STRUCK AGAIN. A young Antillean prostitute was found strangled in her studio on Chapel Street. The lifeless body. . ."

She lifts her gaze, slowly, and looks at him.

This you?

THE MAN: It's me.

THE GIRL: You don't have the face of a killer.

THE MAN: A killer doesn't have a face. If I showed you my chest, you'd see their claws, the marks they left fighting.

   Go.

They look at each other again. She puts on a big smile.

THE GIRL: Death doesn't scare me. See: I'm not afraid.

THE MAN: . . .

She approaches him.

THE GIRL: I've been waiting for so long. Let me do it.

THE MAN: You gotta go.

THE GIRL: Don't say a word.

The man is distraught. She takes his hands tenderly.

THE GIRL: Beautiful. Strong. Rough.
   I want them.

She caresses them; places them on her cheeks; around her neck.

   Do it. I'm begging you. Do it.

The man is totally lost. He lets her guide his hands; his fingers exert pressure.

THE GIRL: Yes. . .

He squeezes harder. She seems relaxed, at ease; she seems to smile. She emits a moan. Her legs double. The man falls with her without letting go of her neck. A large smile overtakes his face.

Offstage, we hear the voice of the girl:

"A star. Like a sun, like a huge, brilliant sun. A gigantic light. So bright. It's beautiful. The closer I get, the more I feel I know it. It's as if a memory deep in my heart woke up, took over my mind: it's delicious. A love-filled sleep. Jeannot. It's him."

The man lets go, finally. The body falls heavily onto the road. The man looks at it for a moment. He smiles, and then he places it on the outline of the corpse, in exactly the same position. He kisses her forehead, props her up, a bit, lifts his collar as if to hide his face.

Music rises.
A song. . .

Lights linger on the corpse. Extremely slowly, darkness envelops everything.

THE DAY MY FATHER KILLED ME
by
Charlotte Boimare
&
Magali Solignat

GUADELOUPE

translation by Amelia Parenteau

Around 11:30 last night, in Dampierre, in the town of Gosier, a family tragedy occurred. Following a lively altercation, a man, a father, shot his son. The 18 year-old young man was shot in the abdomen and is now dead. The man was taken into custody.

THE VOICE: A grandmother.

GRANDMOTHER: Other people's lives don't interest me. Since 5 o'clock yesterday the phone has been ringing off the hook, it's my daughter, my great aunt, a former colleague, even a cousin once removed who didn't come to my husband's burial. "Neighbor, neighbor," everyone's exclaiming, everyone's babbling in the stairwell, tététététététététététététététété. It was impossible to dance at my quadrille class last night. Everyone's talking so much about it, all the time, endlessly, carelessly. It's all anyone can talk about. Everyone wants to know what I think, everyone gives their opinion. I don't know, I don't have an opinion, I keep my thoughts to myself. But where there's smoke, there's fire. Psssitt. I couldn't even dance at my quadrille class last night. I'd practiced my steps all week long. My skirt was brand new. I'd put on some of my new perfume that I'd bought at the Destreland Carrefour. My hat was perched perfectly on my head. I was standing in front of my dance partner, who's my favorite lead. And I couldn't dance. Like me, everyone had seen the ticker that runs across the bottom of the television screen during Carnaval on Guadeloupe 1, "Béranger from NRG killed his son." I couldn't dance. I don't even like to talk about other people, it doesn't interest me. It seems the kid had it coming. Keyholes, door frames, binoculars, mouse holes, spyglasses, hallway noises, it's none of my business, it's not very interesting. But if you can't stand the heat, get out the kitchen. Even my dance partner, who is my favorite lead, started to open his mouth. I thought he was going to kiss me, but he just told me about the radio star and the story with his son. I don't like to talk about people, it doesn't interest me. But after what happened, there's certainly something to be said. I went home to dance alone, and he just kept gossiping. He didn't even see me home, psssitt. . . It might rain tomorrow, I don't know. Psssitt. . . I have nine grandkids.

THE VOICE: This is the story of Roméo, also known as Black Bird, a week before his eighteenth birthday. Roméo decided to call himself Black Bird after hearing the Beatles song.

"Black Bird" by The Beatles plays.

He's a dance music choreographer and dancer. His parents met in Cuba and immediately fell in love, particularly his mother. His father made promises of eternal love. Roméo, or Black Bird, was born nine months later. His mother was an OBGYN and she loved him so much... His father didn't see him till he was 16. It was at the Aimé Césaire airport in Fort de France. He hadn't seen him since, but he wished him a happy new year every year over WhatsApp. And every night Roméo—or Black Bird—listened to Béranger—or his father—on *Disrespect* on NRG. A week before his eighteenth birthday, he decided to go live with his father for the first time.

Béranger, his father, live on NRG.

BÉRANGER: Throw the baby out with the bathwater, Papa's here, and you're listening to Disrespect. We have two hours to kill together, so get your right hand ready, today I want to get hard. Jim Morrison, "The End," that means "la fin" in French for you dummies. *Disrespect*.

Music starts.

THE VOICE: Zak, Black Bird's best friend, in the middle of taking an order at McDonald's.

ZAK: (*To the cop*) Would you like a large fries with that Big Mac? (*To himself, in shock*) Dude, what the fuck'd you do?

THE COP: Yes, and a large Coke. We've got a real nightmare tonight at work. Béranger from NRG.

ZAK: (*To the cop*) I know, I'm friends with his son.

THE COP: Not anymore you aren't. He zapped him.

ZAK: (*To himself*) Fathers are no good for nothing, bro. Fathers are just sperm donors.

THE COP: Barbecue sauce with the fries. He loves that.

ZAK: (*To himself*) What the fuck'd you do, dude?

THE COP: Sir, hello, hello!!

ZAK: (*To himself*) Just because he fucked your mother for six months doesn't make him your father.

THE COP: Ma'am, excuse me, this kid is freaking out.

ZAK: (*To himself*) I'm a one-night stand kid, bro. My father's just a donor.

THE COP: Hey! Hello!

ZAK: Yeah, that's the deal. A donor and bam, a shower of welfare checks. At least things are clear.

THE COP: OK, get the employee of the month, please.

ZAK: (*To himself*) No feelings. Your father is the state.

THE COP: Hurry up, there's a bunch of fans in front of the police station tonight and we've got to take care of everything.

ZAK: (*To himself*) It's just like with women, both have to want it. Your father didn't want it. Your father didn't love you.

Hey it's Black Bird, leave me a message.

Hey it's Black Bird, leave me a message.

Hey it's Black Bird, leave me a message.

Hey it's Black Bird, leave me a message.

Silence.

What the fuck'd you do, dude?

As Marivaux said in *The Game of Love and Chance*, we can't force somebody to love us.

He never wanted you to call him Dad, he thought it made him sound old. I knew it wasn't going to work out.

To the line.

Next guest.

THE VOICE: On Facebook, Black Bird writes to Zak, his best friend.

BLACK BIRD: My dad has a guitar-shaped pool. I'm pretty sure his house cleans itself.

THE VOICE: On Facebook, Black Bird writes to his mother.

BLACK BIRD: Here safe. You can send me the 200 Euro wire.

THE VOICE: On Facebook, Black Bird writes to Zak.

BLACK BIRD: He was so surprised to see me, he didn't even remember my name. He'd just got up, he was still getting his head straight.

THE VOICE: On Facebook, Black Bird writes to his mother.

BLACK BIRD: I love you. I think it's gonna work out.

THE VOICE: On Facebook, Black Bird writes to Zak.

BLACK BIRD: Hey bro, he has a home studio. Oh yeah, when you're in show biz, you got no problems, life is great. I was right to come. Nothing but label clothes, Lacoste sunglasses, you rich, you handsome, you get with all these girls, you got a James Bond car, a hunting rifle up on the wall, you can give money to Haiti, you can build a school in Africa. You got a place in St. Barts with a guitar-shapedpool. You can even buy a baby from the Philippines on Amazon. LOL. I'm sure my dad never goes grocery shopping, when he's hungry, he just has to open his mouth. I'm lucky. I think it's gonna work out.

THE VOICE: The cop, Béranger's best friend.

THE COP: A friend is for life. And I won't let you down, man. I'm the first one he called. And he didn't call the police station, he called me on my cell. Normally I'm not allowed to take personal calls at work, but this was my man, so I picked up. "I did something stupid, get here now," is what he told me. Said to myself, this sounds like trouble. Bam, I hopped on my motorcycle. Me and Béranger ride motorcycles together on Sundays. We're part of a group of bikers, that's my family. He could have called Bob or Jean-Pierre, but, well, he called me, that's out of my hands. . . He's my man. And I didn't come back with, "I work for the police," he knows my way of working, I've always covered for him. When I got to his spot, I understood we're not just in trouble, we're screwed. My friend had really fucked up. He told me, "I did something stupid, it went off all by itself." He turned every color in the rainbow, it was like he lost twenty pounds in five minutes. I put my hand on his shoulder and tried to look him in the eyes. He looked mad, he hadn't come down. I told him, "Don't feel guilty, man, everybody loses it sometimes. Let me handle it now. Get yourself a cold beer, and bring me one. Then go comb your hair, you look awful. Give me your shirt, I'm going to put it in my trunk. Fuck, there's blood everywhere. Just don't feel guilty, everybody loses it sometimes." I knew it would go down this way. The kid wasn't mean, he was a sweet, nice kid with a pretty face, but he had no respect. There's plenty of 'em like that, acting like stars even though they're super young. No doubt it's cuz of TV. I don't have any problems with my kid. He understood the rules very young. I kept his mom in line. Maybe a little too much. She left 5 years ago with the kid. Today he's 5 years old, I try not to see him so I don't get attached. Let's be real, kids are a heap of trouble. And I would never be able to take care of my friends like this if I was watching a kid. Béranger, a friend, is for life. I won't let you down, my man. I'm not afraid to say it, when you hit rock bottom, you find out who your real friends are.

THE VOICE: The sound of keys in the lock. It's 3:30 in the morning, Béranger is coming home. Like every night, his face is distorted by rum, disfigured by marijuana, and black and blue from a fist fight. Like every night, it's hard to take off his shoes. Like every night, his motorcycle jacket misses the coat rack. Like every night, he trips on the stairs, falls and shouts.

On Facebook, Black Bird writes to Zoé, his girlfriend.

BLACK BIRD: He just got home. He messed up everything in the house. I thought there was an earthquake, my heart is beating a mile a minute. Are you asleep? What are you wearing? Did you listen to the show tonight?

THE VOICE: Béranger, live on NRG.

BÉRANGER: Get up, lazy bones, Daddy's here, you're listening to *Disrespect*. I'll tell you right away, tonight my underwear's too tight. The first person who calls me, I'm going to break their legs off to get at their goods, this is *Disrespect*. Hello, Priscilla. You're not allowed to just call like that. . . So what's your stupid question? I don't understand, "Should you go to the big house if you see a murder and don't do anything?" Fuck murder, it's all these kids can talk about. We all see murders. I've seen a murder, Géraldine at the switchboard says earlier today, she saw a guy get killed at the bus stop. And she didn't get all worked up. Time for a commercial, hit it, Tony.

DETERGENT AD *(Jingle)*
TO YOU YOU OOH YOU YOU

THE MOTHER: Hi, I'm the mother of the famous four-way assassin. When my son comes home after a long day committing crimes, his clothes are in such a state!

THE COPS: Where are the clothes your son was wearing this evening? At the time when the crime was committed?

THE MOTHER: Here they are. Look how white!

THE COPS: No trace of blood or viscera, it's a miracle.

THE MOTHER: Purex is the miracle!

BÉRANGER: *(Live on NRG)* So Priscilla, you saw a murder? First off, you're innocent, you didn't kill them. . . Also you're not dead, so your mother's not worried. So what's the problem? Oh yeah, you didn't do even the teeny-tiniest thing to help? Damn! Pretty passive! You like it missionary style in bed, right? I'll tell you straight up, it doesn't look good for you. With security cameras now, they'll just show up to accuse you for something you didn't even do. Just like with radar.

Your story sucks, Priscilla, you made me go soft. "Fuck You," Lili Allen. (*Music starts.*) You're listening to *Disrespect*. I mean, soon we're going to have to go buy our packs of cigarettes wearing bulletproof vests.

THE VOICE: Béranger's housekeeper.

THE HOUSEKEEPER: (*Obsessive, a little manic, sexually repressed*) I like it to be clean. I like to clean, when it sparkles, I'm happy. I like a challenge, the dirtier it is, the more I feel alive. At 7 o'clock in the morning, when I open Béranger's door, seeing the state of his living room, I know exactly... My guilty pleasure is cleaning products. I've known Béranger since he was young. Some women collect shoes and bags, for me, it's cleaning products. He's like a son to me. I have them everywhere at my house, in the cupboards, under beds, behind armoires, in the library, in the refrigerator. My brother even hung up shelves for me last Sunday so I could put more in the living room. I have a gift for making even the most stubborn stains disappear. And with Béranger... I'm addicted to the latest, I love finding the rarest gem, I change products every day, when I see ads, I can't help myself. Béranger is generous, I'm not complaining. I don't have an amazing salary, but I'm happy. At any rate, I don't have expensive tastes. His house is kind of my second home. People often ask me if I'm a housekeeper because I like cleaning products or if I like cleaning products because I'm a housekeeper. I can't answer that question, all I know is... It's more like the dirtier it is, the more I feel alive. When he called me last Thursday... I was leaving evening mass with my mother. With cell phones, we're reachable all the time, I'm still not used to it. Béranger has a nice voice... I didn't know it was his son... I like it to be clean. I cleaned everything. There's no trace. I like it to be clean.

THE VOICE: On Facebook, Black Bird writes to Zoé.

BLACK BIRD: It's weird to be in the same house as your dad at night. I think it's going to work out. My father is charismatic. He even has a hunting rifle. He doesn't talk much. He hasn't asked any questions about me since I got here. But we look alike, I have his eyes, his nose and you know the little dimple, above my mouth, he has the same thing, the angel's touch.

THE VOICE: Above our mouths, there's a little vertical indent. In babies, this little dimple is very noticeable. We say when a baby is in its mother's belly, it learns everything, it knows the whole universe, its secrets, love, history, the order of things, and the mysteries of life. When it's born, we say an angel comes to touch its finger to the baby's mouth and sweetly and tenderly tell it, "Shhhhh, hush now, you need to forget everything and learn it all again." And so the baby doesn't know anything anymore, it's born without any knowledge and won't even remember the angel's presence, who's just left one tiny little mark above its mouth.

Zoé, Black Bird's girlfriend.

ZOÉ: My love, my heart's burning. I just ate 11 packages of Kinder Maxi all by myself. My heart's burning, it's good for me. Kinder Maxi is like a drug, you eat 1, then you eat 2, then you eat 11, all the while looking for that first sensation. Remember when I was 13? My parents were gone for the weekend, and you initiated me. On Saturday night, we climbed aboard the *I Have a Dream*, a sailboat at the marina that wasn't even ours. You told me to close my eyes and open my mouth. It wasn't easy to balance on the boat with my eyes closed, I wanted to laugh. When you gently placed a Kinder square on my tongue, I instantly recognized the unmistakable taste of palm oil. It's the same as Nutella. You came close to me, you placed your lips on my lips and we gave each other Kinder kisses. I wanted to throw up. It felt like being grown before I'd grown up. Why aren't you responding to my messages? Where are you? I don't see you on Facebook anymore. When I got back from school on Thursday, my parents were waiting for me in the kitchen, they both had this look. . . They said someone was dead. It was the first time I ever saw my dad cry. They're worried, it's been 3 days since I came out of my room or opened the blinds. I cut off all my hair. Now I really look like Louise Brooks, you're going to love it. It's weird, I dreamed your father killed you. By the way, Julia invited us to a pool party Saturday night, her parents are in St. Barts. I want to make love. My heart's burning. Are my earrings at your place, I can't find them. I feel like I'm grown before I've grown up. I'm not afraid to die, my love. There's a pile of 257 Kinder Maxi wrappers in front of me.

THE VOICE: On Facebook, Black Bird writes to his mother, it's 8:30 pm.

BLACK BIRD: He told me tomorrow he would bring me to the radio station so I could see behind the scenes. I'm so excited. (*Smiley face.*) Right now we're at the Zoo Rock Café in the marina parking lot. It's crazy how many people know him and love him. Everyone talks to him while I have so much to tell him. . . He doesn't introduce me to anyone and he can't even come sit down at the table with me. I eat and eat, I drink and eat, I drink, my stomach hurts. My heart burns. It's going to be okay. Thanks for the wire transfer. I love you.

THE VOICE: Pascale Roc.

PASCALE ROC: It's the same thing every time, when I have a hair appointment the next day, I can't go to sleep. I toss, I turn, I smoke cigarettes.

THE VOICE: A friend of Black Bird's mother.

PASCALE ROC: But tomorrow I can't skip the appointment, it's the anniversary of his death. I can't stand when I get my hair washed and it comes out in handfuls, that's stress, and then with my curls, it takes ages. I need a smoke. It's the stress. . . All the jackuls' comments come back to me, I mean jackals, what do I know, I'm no Webster, at any rate all the stupid shit she hears all day long. I'm not a mother, that's my choice. . . I could have had 3 or 4 kids but. . . What's good is that I can keep smoking weed. I would've already killed myself, if I was her.

WOMAN 1: Life goes on.

PASCALE ROC: I need a smoke.

WOMAN 2: You didn't see him very often anyways.

PASCALE ROC: I want a smoke.

WOMAN 3: You can take care of yourself now.

PASCALE ROC: I would like a smoke.

WOMAN 4: You don't look well, you need magnesium.

PASCALE ROC: It's midnight, fuck, I'm out of smokes.

WOMAN 4: You're still upset about that? But it's been almost a year! You're not getting depressed, are you?

PASCALE ROC: Do they sell smokes online?

WOMAN 5: He was cute, too.

PASCALE ROC: I need a smoke.

WOMAN 6: You're really self-absorbed right now, you're not listening to other people.

PASCALE ROC: I need a smoke.

WOMAN 7: You shouldn't blame frustration. . .

PASCALE ROC: I need a smoke.

WOMAN 7: Stop seeing the glass half empty!

PASCALE ROC: I need a smoke.

WOMAN 7: You have other kids, you have to hang onto them.

PASCALE ROC: I need a smoke.

WOMAN 8: I don't want to see you right now, I don't like it when you're unhappy.

PASCALE ROC: They sell smokes at Zoo Rock.

THE BANKER: Show me the deceased's will and I will cut off the credit card right away.

PASCALE ROC: But I can't go there.

THE BANKER: I can't close the account without your son's signature.

PASCALE ROC: I need a smoke.

THE BANKER: Dead or not dead.

PASCALE ROC: I really need a fucking smoke.

WOMAN 9: And then, let's be honest, he was a difficult child. . .

PASCALE ROC: I need a smoke. I need a smoke. (*Ad lib "I need a smoke" into a frenzy. Then a deep breath.*) But I stopped a month ago, it would be stupid to cave. Tomorrow, for the anniversary of his death, I'll put on a patch.

THE VOICE: On Facebook, Black Bird writes to his mother. It's 1:00 o'clock in the morning.

BLACK BIRD: I want to talk to him, but I'm afraid he's going to yell at me. He's looked right through me all night. I think I'm going to throw up. But don't worry, Mom, it's going to be alright. I love you.

THE VOICE; Coming back to Béranger's, or his father's, place after dinner at the Zoo Rock Café, Roméo, or Black Bird, had thrown up, thrown up so much there was nothing left to throw up. He fell asleep in the middle of the living room, in his disappointment. The next morning, Béranger, or his father, stepped over him to open the rounded bay window and turn on the vacuum in the guitar-shaped pool. He demanded Black Bird clean up the living room and sent him to his room. Laid out all day, unable to sleep and unable to move, he only found the energy to get up when his father, or Béranger, shut the door to the house to go to the radio station. Then he went down into the kitchen and ate a microwaveable Croque Monsieur. All alone. Like an idiot. He asked himself what he would do today. All alone. Like an idiot. He then had the brilliant idea to take his father's weed and go sell it in front of the Gosier post office. All alone. Like an idiot.

A politician visiting his mistress, a week before the regional elections.

THE POLITICIAN: As Plato said, "When fathers get used to letting their children run free, when sons no longer heed their words, when masters tremble before their students and prefer to flatter them, and

finally, when the young no longer obey the laws because they don't recognize anyone or anything's authority over them, then that, in all its beauty and all its youth, is the beginning of tyranny."
(*To her*) My chauffeur is waiting, I have 10 minutes to make you come.
(*To himself*) Today we should demonstrate compassion and solidarity. Upon my and the prefect's decision, we have ordered an uncompromising investigation.
(*To her*) You excite me.
(*To himself*) I'm sending thoughts to the victim and his mother.
(*To her*) I dreamed about fucking you all night long,
(*To himself*) His father, his aunt, his aunties,
(*To her*) I love your skin,
(*To himself*) His brothers and sisters, his half-brothers and half-sisters, his quarter-brothers and quarter-sisters, his great-grandparents,
(*To her*) I can't screw up.
(*To himself*) His preschool peers,
(*To her*) You smell good.
(*To himself*) His elementary school, middle school, and high school peers, not to mention all his neighbors,
(*To her*) You drive me crazy,
(*To himself*) His friends and his allies.
(*To her*) Take off your skirt, it's annoying.
(*To himself*) With 45 murders committed in 2015,
(*To her*) That's good,
(*To himself*) Guadeloupe is France's most dangerous territory.
(*To her*) Turn over.
(*To himself*) I won't remain helpless in the face of violence that is difficult to fight.
(*To her*) I like your hips.
(*To himself*) We need at least 70 more detectives and police officers to reduce crime on the island.
(*To her*) That's pretty, who's it from?
(*To himself*) Faced with such a tragedy, Guadeloupe needs to be strong,
(*To her*) I want to hurt you,
(*To himself*) It should be strong, and the regional authorities should be strict.
(*To her*) Like me.

(*To himself*) We will be. I want to take this opportunity to thank the police force
(*To her*) You like to be spanked, huh?
(*To himself*) who accomplished this extraordinary job.
(*To her*) Shhhh.
(*To himself*) I would especially like to thank Moule's commissary,
(*To her*) Relax.
(*To himself*) the Petit-Bourg firefighters,
(*To her*) Keep the rhythm.
(*To himself*) the Abymes urban area, always on top of things, the community,
(*To her*) Oh!
(*To himself*) the South Basse-Terre communes, and Colombo insurance, official partners of my campaign,
(*To her*) Oh, right there!!!!!
(*To himself*) My Guadeloupe is in pain. Let's fight together against obesity, don't forget to eat 5 fruits and vegetables a day. Next Sunday, vote for a Guadeloupe that's right in the head, a Guadeloupe that feels good in her skin, a Guadeloupe standing on her own two feet.
(*To her*) See you Thursday, my dear.
(*He sings "La Gwadloup ka pâti".*)
"La Gwadloup ka pati adan movè direction, si nou pa fè attention ti mon an ou ké fin an la ri a seize ans. . . "

THE VOICE: Like an idiot, in a seedy room of the Pointe-à-Pitre station, Black Bird waits in custody for Béranger, or his father. All alone. Like an idiot. He got arrested with 14 grams on him. It's 9:00 pm, he nods off. 10:20, 10:22, 10:23. Béranger, drunk, enters the station. He's like a fish in water. He greets the officers, congratulations, bursts of laughter. Glasses clink, frank and virile friendship. In the blink of an eye, four bottles of wine and 20 grams of weed later, Béranger soothes his friends and frees his son. Barely out of the station, Béranger knocks Black Bird down the stairs with a huge kick in the ass. Black Bird gets up, and Béranger punches him in the nose, picks him up by the collar, pushes him against the wall and shouts at him. Black Bird grabs his father by his arms and holds him off. Béranger tries to get free by spitting in his face. Black Bird gently places his head on his father's shoulder. With his arms dangling, Béranger, surprised, stays immobile. After an absent moment he regains his spirits, grabs his son by the collar and drags him to the car.

On Facebook, Black Bird writes to his mother.

BLACK BIRD: Dad is quite a character. I don't know if I want to be like him. . . He still hasn't brought me to the radio station. . . I still haven't told him I recorded a single, but it's just a question of timing. It would be a dream if one day he would play it on his show. It's cool. It's going to work out, Mom. I love you.

THE VOICE: On Facebook, Black Bird writes to Zak.

BLACK BIRD: I want to come home. I'm not sure this is going to work out, man.

THE VOICE: A visual artist.

A VISUAL ARTIST: (*Free-associating, like Salvador Dalí*) I like life. I like death. For me, death doesn't exist. A canvas in progress that will be shown at the Basse-Terre prefecture in the fall. What could be more philosophical, psychoanalytical, psychedelic, eco-political-biblical, than to decide to kill your own son? Many people say off-hand, in a moment of anger, or simply when they're impatient, "I want to kill you, she's going to kill me, I could have killed him, if I had killed him, I kill you, you're killing me with that goatee, etc, etc. . . " But few people do it. He did what he said. He said what he did. In addition, I'm making the decision to do it for you, because I'm your father. Implicitly, I'm showing you an example. Subliminally, I'm not like all those gay fathers who kill themselves in a symbolic manner, you understand, with their sons who want to take their progenitor's power. Sigmund Freud could turn over in his grave, all this is so boring I could cry, and I am bawling, my nose is running. It's no wonder art is dead, dead is as a doornail, so sterile these past few years. I made love with the earth. I said it loud and clear, I am going to shit on this canvas. No interior made exterior, like the work of my intensely academic contemporaries. I put the shit back inside, like the infant who goes back to their uterine home. Yes, I mean the uterus, not to be confused with the placenta, which, by the way, contemporary artists are now eating, pan-fried. Far from the epidurals of a sterile world afraid of suffering, this man braved the taboos of our society. It's an act of generosity to throw his son to the wolves of his amateur pornography audience. That's how he gets closer to God. Didn't God brave taboos to cleanse men of their sins by sacrificing his own son, Jesus, for those who didn't know him, for all, A-L-L the sins of humanity? Simply said, Béranger, by killing on high he who others kill on low, annihilates the destructive compulsion that lies dormant in each of us, in you, in you towards us, in you towards me. I want to poop.

THE VOICE: Béranger, live on NRG.

BÉRANGER: To all the ladies out there who aren't wearing any panties tonight, to all the tiny asses, to all the fat asses, to all the sluts who own it, I'm raising my glass high and I'm drinking it down. The world pains me, you're listening to *Disrespect*. Here's a little dick who was just sobbing in his father's skirts: José. You're a wetback? Are you eating beans again? I'm just saying. Hey José, this isn't the Dollar Store where you get your this and that, with your little dick in one hand and your knife in the other. Go suck on your mama's tit, and stop tying up the whorehouse switchboard. Loser! The next caller better be more interesting! So, who is it? Jennifer? Hmm, smells like a g-string! Let's have an ad, Tony, send in the clowns! I'm going to have a quick chat with Jennifer. Daddy's here, this is *Disrespect*.

Préservex Advertisement.

JEAN-CLAUDE: Did you know Françoise had a baby behind my back?

MICHEL: (Laughs) Ha ha! You still have that problem? I use Préservex with Martine. A condom lubricated with palm oil. Zero percent risk, 100 percent pleasure. And I can sleep well at night. So, who's the father?

JINGLE: With Préservex, no more unpleasant surprises, no more anxious pregnancy tests, men take back control. For their greatest pleasure.

Laughs.

BÉRANGER: (*Live on NRG*) Okay, so let's be real, Jennifer, he's cheating on you. But don't worry, my dear, your man has you under his skin. As Spinoza said, "Certain men love their wives so much, they help themselves to other peoples' to avoid wearing theirs out." I'll let you think on that one. And tell your guy to put a Préservex on the end of his dick when he goes out to copulate with a lady friend in the moonlight. "Voulez-vous coucher avec moi ce soir?" Lady Marmalade. That means take your panties off, I'm calling the shots. (*Music starts.*) You're listening to *Disrespect*. Yes, Jennifer, if you don't want your man to be paying child support all over Guadeloupe, he needs to use Préservex. Let's go, 2 free Préservex for the first faggot who calls. Isn't life beautiful? Next, they're going to say I'm homophobic. *Disrespect*.

THE VOICE: Jennifer, the aesthetician.

JENNIFER: I haven't gotten out of bed in 2 days. I can't even bring the kids to school anymore. My oldest daughter makes food for everyone. My name is Jennifer. I've been called Jennifer for the past year and a half. My mother named me Sylvie but for him, I'm Jennifer. The first time, the first time I was on the radio, I told him, "I'm Sylvie." "That's ugly," he said, "Sylvies are cold. . . You have the right voice to be called Jennifer." I've been fighting to change my name on my ID for the past year and a half. It takes all my energy. I stopped going to driving school. He has a motorcycle, anyways. I told my mother we're together and she didn't believe me. One day he came to pick me up after his radio program. I heard the sound of his motorcycle from a distance. I came down the stairs 4 at a time. The kids? Not an issue. Tia is 8 years old, she can take care of the house all by herself. And they sleep through the night, so they don't even realize I'm not there. I got on behind him. I pressed my breasts against his back. We didn't say a word. I haven't gotten out of bed in 2 days. I can't even bring the kids to school anymore. I don't hear his voice anymore, I can't call him at the radio at night anymore, I don't know my own name. Why did his son do this to us? I know my man, he wouldn't hurt a fly. The kid must really have pushed him over the edge, because things don't happen like that in real life. . . And who has to suffer? Me! If his mother had known how to control him, we wouldn't be here. My man gets out on Sunday. I'm going to wear my jean shorts, yellow platform sneakers, g-string, my pink bustier on top. . . Oh no, I'm going to wear Tia's dress she got for her birthday. It's too big for her. I'll wait for him in front of the station. I'll have my baby in my arms, and Tia will carry a suitcase with everything we own in it. All four of us will get on the motorcycle, and we'll set off into our real life. My baby's name is Béranger. Like Béranger.

THE VOICE: On Facebook, Black Bird writes to Zoé.

BLACK BIRD: I fucked up tonight. I wish I was in your arms. What are you wearing? I would love to have a Kinder Maxi right now. With you. In one week it will be 3 years, and I like sharing Kinders with you more and more. I saw the last photo you posted on Facebook. You look like Louise Brooks. You're beautiful. I fucked up tonight. Right now, I wish I was 7 years old, in my bed, because I wasn't allowed to watch TV at night. In bed, all tucked in, I would listen to the music from the silent films my mother would watch in the living room. And I would fall sweetly into my dreams. Did I tell you my mother was a fan of Louise Brooks? When I'm with my dad, people always ask us if I'm his son. We really look like each other. He's always vague. The other day he told a guy I was his intern. I started laughing, and then I wanted to cry at the same time. He tells me that when you're a public figure, you need to keep your private life to yourself. So it's our little secret, just for us. And then it confuses people, because I don't have his name. I fucked up at Zoo Rock tonight. I called him "Dad" in front of everyone. I'm going to come back soon. I love you.

THE VOICE: *News On Edge*, Guadeloupe One's Magazine.

JINGLE: Guadeloupe One, the warmth of our hearts, like sugar cane when it's nice and sweet. Emotion, buzz, fear, murder, rape: *News On Edge*.

JOURNALIST: From sex, to murders, to attacks, but most of all for scoops you send us from your smartphones: you're the ones creating the buzz. Even you, if you witness a mugging, a murder, or even just sexual harassment, call *News On Edge*.

If you're over 18, you too can become a film director by just getting out your cell phone and filming! Filming! Filming! A team of professional editors will help you edit your story. Today we're receiving video from

Richard M in Dampierre, Richard prefers to remain anonymous. Last night, Richard was lucky enough to come across a "celebrity" crime scene while he was walking his dog, Arthur. Serge, roll the tape!

JINGLE: Emotion, buzz, fear, murder, rape: *News On Edge*.

RICHARD M: I would like to remain anonymous because I was supposed to go to work last night, I'm a night watchman, and I lied to my boss saying my grandmother died. After dinner I was exhausted, I wanted to go to bed. Arthur insisted I needed to take him out for a walk even though he had already done his business before I ate dinner. He was barking and jumping, barking and jumping. First, I kicked him in the stomach. And then afterwards I felt bad, it's thanks to him I'm here today. But when you have an animal who barks like that in your ear, you get the leash and you take him out. I opened the door, and he kept barking as if he were saying, "Don't forget your phone." I went down towards the sea and then Arthur stopped directly in front of Béranger's house from NRG. I know it sounds dumb when I say it, but from where I was standing, I couldn't see anything. I thought of your show right away and I said to myself, this is my moment, I won't get this chance again.

JINGLE: Emotion, buzz, fear, murder, rape: *News On Edge*.

RICHARD M: I got behind a bush, I parted the leaves.

JINGLE: Emotion, buzz, fear, murder, rape: *News On Edge*.

RICHARD M: I got out my phone and I filmed and filmed and filmed. . . It's hard to see, but I kept my phone still in my hand without moving, to have a clean image. I took it upon myself, saying now is my moment, I won't get this chance again.

JINGLE: Emotion, buzz, fear, murder, rape: *News On Edge*.

RICHARD M: Today, barely 24 hours after I recorded it, I'm seeing my film on TV. It's very emotional. Your team is the best.

He gives a thumbs up.

JOURNALIST: Thanks, Richard. . .

RICHARD M: I would like to thank Béranger. . .

JOURNALIST: Thanks, Richard. . .

RICHARD M: His son. . .

JOURNALIST: Thanks, Richard. . .

RICHARD M: And not to mention Arthur, my canine friend.

JOURNALIST: Thanks, Richard, good work. We're all gathered here on stage. Thanks, Richard, these images are sordid. Lots of talent, you knew how to enhance the horror with great lighting. Become a director like Richard in just one day by taking out your phone. Tomorrow, rape in the cafeteria, a film by Géraldine F, only 18 years old. Sensitive souls should abstain. Thanks, Richard, thanks everyone. We'll see you tomorrow, same time, same place, for *News On Edge*.

JINGLE: Emotion, buzz, fear, murder, rape: *News On Edge*.

JOURNALIST: (*Off stage*) Richard, is that an iPhone 6? Oh, a Samsung Galaxy S7! The image is really good!

THE VOICE: That night, at the Zoo Rock Café at the Gosier marina, Béranger was celebrating his 50th birthday. That's the night Black Bird decided the world should know his father had a son. Black Bird was there, sitting in the corner like a piece of furniture. He sipped Ti' Punch after Ti' Punch. That's the night Black Bird decided to come out of the shadows. He watched the group of freeloaders around his father. They were all messed up on booze and cocaine. All his radio coworkers, all the journalists, all his cop friends from the station at Pointe-à-Pitre, all his friends from the Guadeloupe biker federation, all his girlfriends and ex-girlfriends and future girlfriends, all his friends' wives who had passed through his bed, the staff of the Zoo Rock Café; this whole beautiful, obscene group was licking the king of the evening's boots. Swept up in the band of hypocrites, Béranger was full of himself, speaking very loudly, talking to everyone and to no one. Certainly not to his son. At midnight, Black Bird, full of rum, lost it, and tripped the circuit breaker. No more music, everyone was in the dark. Dead drunk, he took a lighter out of his pocket, illuminated his face, and murmured, "Happy Birthday, Dad." No one reacted to his "coming out," the guests were all looking for candles, trying to put the lights back on, using the darkness to fondle each other, and searching through the playlists on their phones to get the party started again. It was as if it never happened. Except for Béranger.

The next day, Béranger was live on NRG.

BÉRANGER: Hey you sons of. . . No cursing on the radio. So let's not talk bad about whores behind their backs when they're taking a thorn out of the foot of humanity. My love to all the Carénage whores working this evening. You're listening to *Disrespect*. Tonight I have a personal attack to talk about. It's not something I usually do, but I'm really pissed about this one. To all you so-called journalists, I'd like to suggest you check your sources, guys. You can do a lot of harm. When I see my face on the front page of your rags with the headline saying, "Daddy Béranger," without even a phone call to a brother to verify the story, that makes me sick. Since you didn't ask for the truth, I'm going to give it to you, this kid is an intern who's doing vocational work hours for his technical degree, ok? He's always up my ass at the radio, ok? I don't know what I mean to him, but he's projecting something onto me, that much is clear. I don't do anything but show him the tricks of the trade, but that's all, that's it, period, end of story. "Love on the Beat," Gainsbarre. (*Music starts.*) You're listening to *Disrespect*. Journalists, do your job, and everything will be ok.

THE VOICE: Black Bird's room on the mezzanine. A big room with walls that must have been white a long time ago. Punch, headbutt, Black Bird hits the wall. Yellow pages and white pages and yellow pages and white pages from the phone book are on the ground. With a dry throat and cloudy eyes, he extends his wrist, covered in blood, towards the ash tray to get his joint. Bundles of free supermarket circular advertisements are on the ground. He nervously takes a drag off his joint and falls asleep, disappointed. Envelopes and bills are on the ground. Encyclopedias and motorcycle magazines. Black Bird wakes up in a sweat.

THE VOICE: A young chef's apprentice.

A YOUNG CHEF'S APPRENTICE: I hate it. I don't know how to say it, ya know? I have too many emotions, I gotta breathe, my mom told me to. Pfffff. . . It hits me right in the gut. These journalist fucks! (*He slaps himself.*) Gotta stop cursing, you know, but I got hate on the tip of my tongue. Journalists are a dirty bunch, they mix you up in the head like they're the ones who know the truth, ya know? They make you believe it's the kid's fault the father pulled the trigger. In the streets, at high school, in the stores, even the doctor, I get there and right away he says, "You have to stop smoking marijuana, Béranger killed his kid because of drugs, he couldn't control it." Yeah right, don't give me that shit, I gotta breathe, my mom told me to. Thankfully I got cooking, ya know? Cooking is my passion. All this rage, all this hate, I put it in a dish, I give it my all. I've been waiting for it to be 6 in the morning for the past 3 hours, ya know? I'm going straight to the market, yo, I'm gonna let my instinct guide me, yo, I'm gonna make a dish, make a dish. I'm dying inside. I want something savory, something bad, something sweet, then all of a sudden it explodes, you don't know what's happening to you, you're in pain, right in the gut. I didn't know you, man, you were my age, brother, you're with me all the time now that you're dead, man. I'm dying inside. The dish I'm gonna make, they're gonna shut up, this hot pepper's gonna make them cry and stop talking into the void. Your father was a son of a. . . (*He slaps himself.*) Gotta stop cursing, ya know, but I've got hate on the tip of my tongue. I'm gonna fight, I'm gonna use my degree, you know what, man, I'm gonna name my dish after you. I did the same thing 7 years ago with my dad. Like a remembrance. I'm dying inside. I miss you, Dad.

THE VOICE: On Facebook, Black Bird writes to Zak.

BLACK BIRD: I had a bad dream, I don't feel good. I was in my underwear in front of the shitty vending machine at the Texaco station. I was looking for 2 euros in my jeans to buy an orange Fanta, even though I was in my underwear. In the vending machine there were only little cans of Fanta, and what was really weird was my mother's face was on each of the little cans. She was looking at me with love. Tap, tap, tap, I felt a finger on my shoulder. It's my father. He's handing me a 2 euro coin. I put it in the slot. A huge bottle falls. It's hot lemon Fanta. I drink straight from the bottle really fast and I hand it to my father. As he drinks, he turns into me. I suffocate. I sweat. My father's hands get closer, I'm paralyzed, they slowly get closer to my neck and they trap me. And then, thankfully, I woke up. I can't wait to get back, I'm waiting for a wire from my mother and I'm buying a ticket.

THE VOICE: On Facebook, Black Bird writes to Zoé.

BLACK BIRD: I just ate a box of 11 Kinder Maxi all by myself. I miss you. I can't wait to come back, I'm waiting for a wire from my mom and I'll buy a ticket.

THE VOICE: Mrs. Béquette.

MRS. BÉQUETTE: (*Upper class, colonial snob*) What an awful day, May 10th. I don't get it. May 10th is the commemorative day in memory of the abolition of slavery. I don't get it. "The whites are bad, they do nothing but hurt us." So the blacks are good, and the whites are bad. . . Isn't that a bit simplistic? When they were slaves, fathers didn't have the right to recognize their sons, and now they kill them, on the commemorative day, to boot. I don't get it. And I know myself, when I don't get something, it bothers me. I can't carry the weight of the world on my shoulders. Yes, it's annoying, he didn't control his temper. Yes, it's awful, he shouldn't have had a firearm at home. Yes, it's sad, he must have been drunk and certainly high. Yes, certain people think it was premeditated. Yes, it's absurd for a father to kill his son, yes yes yes yes, I never said any different. . . We are brought up with racism from the beginning of time. But in this case, they were the same color, no? Luckily the little one died on May 10th, otherwise they might have given us a national day of mourning, too. And then a national day of mourning, that means a day off, and a day off means no cleaning lady, and no cleaning lady means a disgusting house. And then who gets stuck with the housekeeping when black men kill their sons? But of course nobody wants to talk about that.

THE VOICE: In the middle of the afternoon, Black Bird leaves his room. Like a zombie. He drinks a liter and a half of warm lemon Fanta straight from the bottle in the kitchen. Like a zombie. It's May 10th. Tap tap tap, a hand on his shoulder, Black Bird jumps, Béranger is there, addressing him for the first time. Before leaving for the radio, he forbids him to leave the house during the day. Black Bird chokes on warm lemon Fanta, coughs, and spits his mouthful on Béranger's shoes. The door slams, the motorcycle revs, Béranger leaves for the radio. Black Bird feels an irrepressible rage mounting in him. He calls his mother, Zak, and Zoé. No one picks up. He calls his mother, Zak, and Zoé. No one picks up. He goes to the mezzanine, gathers his things, takes his bag, leaves his father's house, and starts to walk. He calls his mother, Zak, and Zoé. No one picks up. He's got anger in his throat, questions in his stomach, and rage in his ears. Legs trembling, his feet not knowing where he's going, his heart is heavy. He turns around and decides to wait for his father in front of the house to get it off his chest. He calls his mother, Zak, and Zoé. No one picks up.

THE VOICE: A tourist couple.

MALE TOURIST: It's a shame you two weren't here last night. We ate a beautiful lobster with red beans and rice.

FEMALE TOURIST: And it wasn't even expensive, it was included in the price for the week.

MALE TOURIST: And then the Planteur Punch, let me tell you. . .

FEMALE TOURIST: Luckily the room wasn't far away!

MALE TOURIST: If I'd had to drive, I would've been headed straight to the drunk tank.

FEMALE TOURIST: However when it comes to the service, you can't be in a rush here, it must be the heat. . .

MALE TOURIST: I came to Guadeloupe on vacation for the beautiful beaches and the *vahinés*. Black women are the most beautiful in the world.

FEMALE TOURIST: It's just too bad they're black. So, what has the chef made for us this evening?

MALE TOURIST: I hope we're not going to eat local every night, because that's not going to work with my stomach. I'm not against exoticism, but they've got to adapt to us a little, too.

FEMALE TOURIST: Yesterday we visited the Basse-Terre market with our group. There were so many colors and smells all mixed together, people talking loudly, drums in our ears.

MALE TOURIST: I haven't done Africa, but it didn't make me want to go there. And here, my friend, they see you coming.

FEMALE TOURIST: Prices depend on what you look like.

MALE TOURIST: The guide told me, "Leave it, Jean-Pierre, give me your wallet and I'll take care of it." Our guide is very nice.

FEMALE TOURIST: She's a dyke.

MALE TOURIST: Oh yeah? And then, all of a sudden at the market, I heard the natives start howling. I said to myself. . .

FEMALE TOURIST: The people from our group were all spread out from here to there, eating *accras*.

MALE TOURIST: I said to myself. . .

FEMALE TOURIST: Buying dolls to put on the TV set. . .

MALE TOURIST: I said to myself. . .

FEMALE TOURIST: Buying pineapples, and limes. . .

MALE TOURIST: Honey, please. I said to myself, "Jean-Pierre, something is happening. Leave the group, you're not a sheep." The Guadeloupeans were in front of the tribunal and they were singing at full volume to a song by Zouk Machine. "Liberate Béranger, Gwada is more than proud of you." I asked around who this Béranger was, and they said he was a local celebrity who had killed his son.

FEMALE TOURIST: Yes. . .

MALE TOURIST: So, my friend, that certainly spiced up my vacation! All swept up in it, I started to sing with them, "Liberate Béranger, Gwada..." I clapped my hands and I felt like a local, I felt like I was black. Then that night at the hotel, sitting in front of my 500 gram lobster, my European side came back, and I thought about it.

FEMALE TOURIST: It is strange to be celebrated when you've killed your son.

MALE TOURIST: I asked the waiter if it was a local custom. He was surprised and didn't know how to answer me. I asked the guide, the dyke, and she told me, "Leave it, Jean-Pierre, don't think too hard about it, you're on vacation." And so I held my questions and went to karaoke.

FEMALE TOURIST: When we got back to the room, you puked all night.

MALE TOURIST: I threw up so much there wasn't anything left to throw up.

THE VOICE: Black Bird enters the house in a rage. He turns on the radio, it's Béranger's program.

BÉRANGER: (*Live on NRG*) Today it's Daddy's treat, two kebabs with fries at the Zoo Rock Café for the first asshole to call Géraldine at the switchboard and tell us what we celebrate on May 10th. Careful, no jokes below the waist, Géraldine has a very jealous husband. Me, on the other hand, I don't have a wife, I don't have any kids, and I love dirty jokes. This is *Disrespect*.

THE VOICE: Black Bird, in the living room like a lion in his cage, grabs the Sony 3D gold-plated flat-screen TV and throws it in the guitar-shaped pool. He delights in watching the TV drown in the pool's depths.

BÉRANGER: (*Live on NRG*) You lose, Yohann, May 10th isn't just the commemorative day for the abolition of slavery in France. It's also the day of Saint Solange, whom we forget all too often under Taubira's reign. "I Want Your Sex," George Michael. (*Music starts.*) You're listening to *Disrespect*. If your name is Solange, call me. Tonight, I'm celebrating you.

THE VOICE: Black Bird shuts off the radio. He throws it against the bay window. It shatters. Pieces of glass go everywhere. The radio strains, we hear Béranger's voice die out little by little. Standing agitated, in a sweat, before the open door to the fridge, he downs a liter of lemon Fanta in one gulp. Everything is a jumble in his head: leave right away, stay, go to the radio station, set the house on fire, stay, talk to him, wait for him with a baseball bat to break his teeth, eat a microwavable Croque Monsieur, hang himself from the ceiling fan, scream, explode, buy a new flat-screen TV at Conforama. Finally, he decides to stay put in the living room to talk to him. His fear mounts, he glances at the rifle with a feeling of insecurity, something non-rational, the feeling of being in danger. He takes a small knife from the kitchen, the first one he sees, a table knife, impulsively, to calm his nerves. He calls his mother, Zak, and Zoé. No one picks up.

THE VOICE: A little 6 1/2 year-old boy.

THE LITTLE BOY: Mama says I have to tell my nightmare to my s'rink. She says the s'rink can take away all my fears, even the ones from when I was a baby and the ones from when I'm grown up. I can't sleep. I'm afraid he's going to come and steal me. Mama and Papa tell me it's not possible and they'll protect me, he can't come in the house, and in any case we have an alarm on the door that is directly linked to the police, Mama and Papa told me. Thursday, somebody stole my teacher's bike even though she had a bike lock on it. It seems like with a 2 euro coin, you can open the door of the school linked to the police. It seems like the police, they say they're police but they aren't really police. I'm afraid he's going to come take me away. He lives just across the street from us. He only has to cross the road and break down the door, it's easy because it's made of wood. Mama says there's iron inside to protect us and the wood around it is just to make it look nice. But I don't believe her. I don't like curse words, I'm afraid, I love motorcycles. He promised he would take me on a ride on his motorcycle and we would hit on girls. He has big hands, a big head, and big shoes. I'm little. How old do you have to be to kill a child? I don't want to ride on a motorcycle anymore. I haven't slept in 2 days, I looked out the window. On the neighbor's patio, at the neighbor's house, there were police officers and the neighbor and they were all drinking beer. It seemed like they were police officers, they said they were police officers, but they weren't really police officers. I wish he'd've stayed in prison. This morning Mama and Papa told me we're going to move.

THE VOICE: The gravel crunches, an alcoholic skid, Béranger shouts and laboriously picks up his motorcycle. The sound of keys in the lock. It's 10:47 pm. Tonight he's high on weed, his face bashed in by a jealous husband. He's rum-drunk. Béranger sees Black Bird in the ruins of his living room. He shouts and smashes the coffee table with his fist, which breaks in two, he's hot, he wants a fight. Black Bird curls up on the couch. Béranger grabs him by the belt, Black Bird resists and kicks him in the stomach, Béranger falls in the shards of glass. In a fit, Black Bird throws himself on him, says with his blows the words he could never speak and in a single breath, he beats him up, strikes him in the chest and in the face, a round of punches. Béranger defends himself as well as he is able. His brow runs with blood, his nose is broken, and his breath is stifled. He manages to get up, despite Black Bird's significant force. Béranger plucks Black Bird off his chest and throws him into the guitar-shaped pool. Black Bird swallows water and chokes. Béranger sips the end of a bottle of rum that's lying on the bar to get his head straight. Eyes burning with chlorine, exhausted, and weak, but still with fire in his belly, Black Bird gets out of the pool. Like a bull, with his head lowered, he charges straight at his father. He slips on pieces of broken glass, cuts himself trying to get back up, and sees his father get the rifle from above the couch. Panicked, he crawls feebly towards the door and manages to stand back up, holding his little knife tightly in his pocket, and runs to escape...

A long silence, time is suspended.

THE VOICE: Angel Gaby.

ANGEL GABY: What are you still doing here? Got to go now. It's time to leave, get in the car, Simone! What is your name, though? Black Bird? The Beatles! I'm their biggest fan. I was at their last concert in '66 in San Francisco, caviar for the ears! And then, who brought John Lennon upstairs in 1980? Yours truly! I swear, that was the big time, Saint Peter was eating out of my hand. Ever since, I've been resting on my laurels a bit, I don't really want to work anymore. Let's go young man, you can't stay here! I'm making mistake after mistake,

I'm not concentrating. Take Michael Jackson, he died when? In 2009! Well, I still haven't succeeded with that sinner, he floats, he laughs at me, he appears, he disappears, he doesn't give a flying fuck about me. I'm losing points. Hello soul-taker, here's a fallen angel! Saint Peter's radical, if I don't bring him up in the next two years, it's my retirement, honey. Do you have a smoke? No, forget about it, we've gotta go. I want to get sealed up again. A clean spirit in a clean body. What time is it? Fuck, I've got no sense of time, leave your watch, by the way. And your cell phone, we don't have 3G up there anyways. In the beginning it's tricky, but don't say I told you. But in terms of your spirit, bam, you arrive straight on chakra 12. You travel light, huh? Underwear, a toothbrush, and you're good to go. You have any food allergies? Pillow or bolster? Sweet or savory? You believe in God? Honestly, I have no idea. . . He's always shut up in his office or out on a call. Totally inaccessible, that guy! Okay, let's go, sweetie, I'm gonna get in trouble. He shot you in the back, that dick?! Hey, seriously, since Greek myths, I've never seen anything like that. The last to date was Zeus. Well done, my man! Ah no, it was Marvin Gaye. You're already a star, a kid who's killed by his own father, that gets you points right away. They're waiting for you up there, c'mon, let's go, big guy, say goodbye to everyone. This reminds me of your first day of preschool. You were brave that day. Come on, take a deep breath, we'll count to 3 and then you let everything go. 1, 2. . . It seems like you rip a little guitar, they're all waiting for you up there, there's Jimmy, John, Jim, and Bob. They're great, those guys.

"Black Bird" by The Beatles plays.

BLACK BIRD: That's the story of Roméo, or Black Bird, a week before his 18th birthday. Roméo decided to call himself Black Bird while listening to The Beatles' song.

END OF PLAY

About the Playwrights

Charlotte Boimare was born in 1976 in Paris where she trained as an actor. In addition to her work in film and television, she worked in theater with Dario Fo, Franca Rame, Jean-Luc Moreau, Christophe Botti, and Michel Laliberté.

Daniely Francisque was born in 1972 in Martinique and grew up as a child in the suburbs of Paris. After studying languages and cultural management, she turned to the arts and trained as an actor, singer, and dancer. Besides her film work, she also appeared on stage in over forty theatre and dance productions in France and in the Caribbean. After returning to Martinique in 2010, she founded her own theater company TRACK, exploring movement on stage.

Jean-René Lemoine was born in Haiti in 1959. He is a French-Haitian playwright who lives in Paris. Trained as an actor in Paris and Brussels, he is the author of ten plays which were awarded several prizes, including the Fondation Beaumarchais and the Académie Française awards. Lemoine's works have been staged in national theaters in Paris (Comédie Française, Cartoucherie, Théâtre de la Ville).

Gaël Octavia was born in 1977 in Martinique, and is currently living in Paris. She is an interdisciplinary artist who writes, paints, and creates short films. Influenced by the Martinican environment where she grew up, she takes up universal themes such as migration, class, race, and the place of women in society in her artistic works. She is the author of award-winning plays that were staged and/or read in France, the US, and the Caribbean.

Guy Régis Jr was born in 1974 in Haiti. He is a dramatist, novelist, poet, director, actor, video maker and has translated Camus and Proust in Creole. In 2001 he founded the company NOUS Théâtre (WE Theater) which promotes a political and experimental physical theatre. His plays have been staged in the Caribbean, Europe, Africa, and South America. After directing the Theater Studies Department of the National School of the Arts in Port-au-Prince, Haiti, he is now the director of the Festival 4 Chemins which promotes the development of performing arts in Haiti.

Luc Saint-Éloy was born in Djibouti in 1955. He trained as an actor and director in France. Since 1983, he has been the director of the Théâtre de l'Air Nouveau in Paris. Deeply engaged in the African-Caribbean arts in France, Saint-Éloy is also the head of the Centre Culturel pour la Promotion des Arts Afro-Caraïbes. He has directed over 20 performances in which he revisits the history of colonialism and slavery, combining theater, music, dance, and storytelling.

Magali Solignat, born in France in 1976, worked for many years in Guadeloupe as an actor, director, and by conducting theater workshops in schools. Besides her work in theatre with José Pliya and Jacques Martial, she has worked in film with Peter Watkins.

About the Translators

Josh Gray Cohen is an essayist, translator, historian, and occasional actor living in New York. He is currently completing his Ph.D. in the Committee of the Study of Religion at Harvard University.

Danielle Carlotti-Smith is a writer, scholar, and an adjunct professor of comparative literature at the University of Tulsa in the Global Scholars Program. She also serves as a Research Fellow at the Oklahoma Center for the Humanities. Carlotti-Smith earned her Ph.D. in French at the University of Virginia. She specializes in French and Francophone literature, culture, and film, with a focus on Francophone Caribbean and the New World Studies, postcolonial studies, and migration studies.

Amanda Gann is a theater artist and Ph.D. candidate at Harvard University. Her current work, at the intersection of performance and research, focuses on social and theatrical manifestation of grief in post-WWI France as well at the question of affect in historical inquiry. Trained as an actress in France, the US, and most recently the UK (MFA, East 15), she collaborates as a performer with international companies such as the Poets' Theater. She has worked as a literary translator and interpreter for the French Theatrical Foundation and the Harvard Film Study Center.

Judith Graves Miller is Professor of French and Collegiate Professor at New York University, where she has also served as Chair of the French Department and Dean of Arts and Humanities at New York University Abu Dhabi. She has published numerous articles on French and Francophone theatre (text and production) and has translated some twenty-five plays (including works by Hélène Cixous, Werewere Liking, José Pliya, Koffi Kwahulé, Bernard-Marie Koltès, and Olivier Kemeid). Her latest books include an anthology of plays by Ivoirian Koffi Kwahulé (*Seven plays by Koffi Kwahulé: In and Out of Africa*, Michigan, 2017), a translation of Guadeloupian artist Gerty Dambury's novel *Les Rétifs* (*The Restless*) for the Feminist Press, 2018; and a translation of Béatrice Picon-Vallin's prize-winning study of the Théâtre du Soleil, Routledge, 2020.

Amelia Parenteau is a freelance writer, translator, and theatermaker based in New Orleans with a focus on Equity, Diversity, and Inclusion. An alumna of Sarah Lawrence College, she has worked with TCG, Ping Chong + Company, The Lark, The Civilians, The French Institute Alliance Française, Voyage Theater Company, and the Park Avenue Armory in New York; People's Light in Pennsylvania; The Eugene O'Neill Theater Center in Connecticut; and Théâtre du Soleil in France. She has translated dramatic works by Leslie Kaplan, Alain Foix, Sedef Ecer, the Théâtre du Soleil, and David Lescot. She is a member of the FENCE International Translation Network, ATALS, and TCG, and has been published in several magazines and journals including *American Theatre Magazine*, *Asymptote Literary Magazine*, *Contemporary Theater Review*, *Culturebot*, *HowlRound*, and *The Mercurian*.

Lucie Tiberghien is a French and American director who has called Brooklyn her home since 2002. Specializing in the development of new plays, she has directed world premieres in New York and all over the country. She is also the founder and artistic director of Molière in the Park, a Brooklyn based nonprofit dedicated to bringing Free, Inclusive theater to Prospect Park in Brooklyn, on a yearly basis.

Kate Woff graduated from the University of Virginia in 2014, where she translated *Une vie familiale* as part of her distinguished Major Project thesis. Following a Master's degree in Global Shakespeare at Queen Mary University of London and Warwick University, she spent time working for the British Council in rural Picardy. Kate has since trained as a primary school teacher in her native London, where she now teaches in an inner-city primary school.

About the Editor

Stéphanie Bérard (Ph.D. University of Minnesota/Université de Provence) is a specialist of Francophone Caribbean and African theater and has taught in the US, Canada, and France. She is currently a Senior Lecturer in French at the American University of Paris. Her research is situated at the crossroads of Postcolonial and Theater Studies, exploring the history of Caribbean drama, Creole and French, oral tradition, rituals, and drum music and dance. She is the author of *Théâtres des Antilles : traditions et scènes contemporaines* (2009) and *Le Théâtre-Monde de José Pliya* (2015) and she co-edited *Emergences Caraïbes, une création théâtrale archipélique* (2010). She was awarded an NEH Fellowship for her project on Haitian drama, and a Marie Curie European Fellowship for FACT (Francophone African and Caribbean Theaters).

About the Cover Artist

Ronald Cyrille, born to a Dominican mother and a Guadeloupean father, spent his childhood in Dominica before moving to Guadeloupe. He obtained his master's degree in visual arts in 2012 at the Campus Caribéens des Arts de la Martinique and was awarded the "Jam Session" young talent of Martinique and the "Prix Start" of the Conseil Départemental de la Guadeloupe in the visual arts category. The in-between is a constant for this artist who practices Street art (as B-Bird) and who is close to both hip-hop culture and West Indian tales. In his paintings, drawings, and collages, he brings together figures of a real and imaginary bestiary. He appropriates the photographer's technique before diverting it and adding it to his eclectic studio practice (bombing, scratching, acrylic, posca, collage...). These supports are new places where reality meets imagination to tell stories that borrow from tales and mythologies of the West Indies, and the "magical-religious imagination" of the Creole language.

Caribbean Theatre Project
ACT (Actions Caribéennes Théâtrales)
Monday + Tuesday
December 2 + 3, 2019
2:00pm Discussion + 4:00pm, 6:00pm, 8:00pm Readings
Segal Theatre
The Graduate Center, CUNY, 365 Fifth Avenue at 34th Street

FREE + Open to the public
First come, first served

The ACT / Actions Caribéennes Théâtrales project is initiated and coordinated by Stéphanie Bérard, specialist in Caribbean Theater, author of *Théâtres des Antilles*, in collaboration with Frank Hentschker from the Martin E. Segal Center at The CUNY Graduate Center, Nicole Birmann Bloom from the Cultural Services of the French Embassy in New York, with Compagnie Siyaj from Guadeloupe, and with the participation of the choreographer/cultural producer Candace Thompson-Zachery as external artistic advisor.

MONDAY, DECEMBER 2

2:00pm

Roundtable: Women and/in Caribbean Theatre

With **Romola Lucas, Amina Henry, Magali Solignat,** and **Charlotte Bomaire**

Moderated by **Candace Thompson-Zachery**

4:00pm

Street Sad / Trottoir Chagrin

Written by **Luc Saint-Éloy** (Guadeloupe)

Translated by **Josh Cohen**

Directed by **Paul Price**

Q&A moderated by **Steve Puig**

A prostitute is walking the streets of Paris. She does not care about anything nor anyone. One evening, she returns to the place where her brother Jeannot was murdered just a year before. There she meets a mysterious man with whom she starts a conversation and enters into a dangerous flirtation.

6:00pm

The Day My Father Killed Me / Le jour où mon père m'a tué

Written by **Magali Solignat** & **Charlotte Boimare** (Guadeloupe)

Translated by **Amelia Parenteau**

Directed by **Florent Masse**

Q&A moderated by **Amélie Parenteau**

Based on a true story of a singer who murdered his son in Guadeloupe. Devised as a documentary theatre work, the play offers a diverse narrative account of the crime and the violence in contemporary Caribbean society.

8:00pm

Adoration / L'Adoration

Written by **Jean-René Lemoine** (Haiti/France)

Translated by **Amanda Gann**

Directed by **Sylvaine Guyot**

Q&A moderated by **Amin Erfani**

In a nightclub on a terrace overlooking the sea, a woman, Chine, and a man, Rodez, reflect on their relationship. Memories of desire, obsession, love, and hate mix with the sounds of the waves they hear from far away. Slowly, Chine unveils the inner workings of a dangerous passion in which she lost herself.

TUESDAY, DECEMBER 3

2:00pm

Roundtable: Caribbean Theatre on the International Stage

With **Luc Saint-Éloy, Daniely Francisque,** and **Oceana James**

Moderated by **Stéphanie Bérard**

4:00pm

Family / Une vie familiale

Written by **Gaël Octavia** (Martinique)

Translated by **Katharine Woff**

Directed by **Lucie Tiberghien**

Q&A moderated by **Nandi Jacob**

A father hides his homosexuality from his family and tries to escape a stifling and suffocating family. The alcoholic stay-at-home mother is jealous of the relationships her husband has with her children. In this average dysfunctional family, everyone struggles playing the social games they are expected to play. The lies, secrets, and silences ultimately blow up the constraining social conventions they lived with before.

6:00pm

And the Whole World Quakes: The Great Collapse / De toute la terre le grand effarement

Written by **Guy Régis Jr** (Haiti)

Translated by **Judith Miller**

Directed by **Kaneza Schaal**

Q&A moderated by **Christian Flaugh**

Two women, survivors of a catastrophe, stand on a hill overlooking a destroyed city. The Youngest and the Oldest look upon the desolated landscape and hear the lamentations, prayers, and songs of the survivors.

8:00pm

She-Devil / Ladjablès

Written by **Daniely Francisque** (Martinique)

Translated by **Danielle Carlotti-Smith**

Directed by **Oceana James**

Q&A moderated by **Andrew Clarke**

During a night of the Carnival Martinique, a female masked dancer meets an arrogant man who tries to seduce her. Drunken by desire, the heartless man does not realize that the predator is slowly becoming the prey of the bewitching dancer.

Plays have been selected by a distinguished advisory board:

Alessandra Benedicty-Kokken (The Graduate Center, CUNY),

Nicole Birmann Bloom (Cultural Services of the French Embassy in New York),

Stéphanie Bérard (specialist in Caribbean Theater, author of Théâtres des Antilles)

Mária Brewer (University of Minnesota),

Heather Denyer (Graduate Center, CUNY),

Amin Erfani (Lehman College, CUNY),

Christian Flaugh (Buffalo University),

Amaya Lainez Le Déan (translator and director, Buenos Aires).

External Artistic Advisor: **Candace Thompson-Zachery.**

Founded in 2002 and directed by Gilbert Laumord and Elvia Gutiérrez in Guadeloupe, **SIYAJ** is a government subsidized theater company supported by the French Ministry of Culture and the Regional Council. SIYAJ asserts a Caribbean identity anchored in popular traditions inherited from Africa (drum rituals, oral tradition, Creole) and favors interdisciplinary aesthetic forms (music, dance, drama). Promoting intercultural collaborations (Cuba, Haiti, and South Korea), Siyaj has produced 10 plays performed in the Caribbean, metropolitan France, Asia, and the US.

The ACT / Actions Caribéennes Théâtrales project is supported by **FACE Contemporary Theater**, a program developed by **FACE Foundation** and the **Cultural Services of the French Embassy in the United States** with the support of the Florence Gould Foundation, the Ford Foundation, Institut français-Paris, the French Ministry of Culture, and private donors.

The translations of *Adoration* by Jean-René Lemoine and *And the Whole World Quakes (The Great Collapse)* by Guy Régis Junior are supported by the CONTXTO network.

All events are FREE and open to the public on a first come, first served basis at The Martin E. Segal Theatre Center, The Graduate Center, City University of New York, 365 Fifth Avenue, at 34th Street.

Subway: Herald Square, lines B/D/F/M/N/Q/R/W

www.theSegalCenter.org Info: 212-817-1860

The Martin E. Segal Theatre Center (MESTC) is a non-profit center for theatre, dance, and film affiliated with CUNY's PhD Program in Theatre and Performance. The Center's mission is to bridge the gap between academia and the professional performing arts communities both within the United States and internationally. By providing an open environment for the development of educational, community-driven, and professional projects in the performing arts, MESTC is a home to theatre scholars, students, playwrights, actors, dancers, directors, dramaturgs, and performing arts managers from the local and international theatre communities.

Through diverse programming—staged readings, theatre events, panel discussions, lectures, conferences, film screenings, dance—and a number of publications, MESTC enables artists, academics, visiting scholars, and performing arts professionals to participate actively in the advancement and appreciation of the entire range of theatrical experience. The Center presents staged readings to further the development of new and classic plays, lecture series, televised seminars featuring professional and academic luminaries, and arts in education programs, and maintains its long-standing visiting scholars-from-abroad program. In addition, the Center publishes a series of highly-regarded academic journals, as well as books, including plays in translation, written, translated, and edited by leading scholars.

www.theSegalCenter.org

The PhD Program in Theatre and Performance, The Graduate Center, CUNY, is one of the leading doctoral theatre programs in the United States. The Faculty includes distinguished professors, holders of endowed chairs, and internationally recognized scholars. The program trains future scholars and teachers in all the disciplines of theatre research. Faculty members edit MESTC publications, working closely with the doctoral students in theatre who perform a variety of editorial functions and learn the skills involved in the creation of books and journals.

www.gc.cuny.edu/theatre-and-performance

The **MESTC Publication Wing** produces both journals and individual volumes. Journals include *Slavic and Eastern European Performance* (SEEP), *The Journal of American Drama and Theatre* (JADT), and *Western European Stages* (WES). Books include *Four Melodramas by Pixérécourt* (edited by Daniel Gerould and Marvin Carlson—both Distinguished Professors of Theatre at the CUNY Graduate Center), *Contemporary Theatre in Egypt*, *The Heirs of Molière* (edited and translated by Marvin Carlson), *Seven Plays by Stanisław Ignacy Witkiewicz* (edited and translated by Daniel Gerould), *The Arab Oedipus: Four Plays* (edited by Marvin Carlson), *Theatre Research Resources in New York City* (edited by Jessica Brater, Senior Editor Marvin Carlson), *Comedy: A Bibliography of Critical Studies in English on the Theory and Practice of Comedy in Drama, Theatre and Performance* (edited by Meghan Duffy, Senior Editor Daniel Gerould), *BAiT-Buenos Aires in Translation: Four Plays* (edited and translated by Jean Graham-Jones), *roMANIA AFTER 2000: Five New Romanian Plays* (edited by Saviana Stanescu and Daniel Gerould), *Four Plays from North Africa* (edited by Marvin Carlson), *Barcelona Plays: A Collection of New Plays by Catalan Playwrights* (edited and translated by Marion Peter Holt and Sharon G. Feldman), *Josep M. Benet i Jornet: Two Plays* (edited and translated by Marion Peter Holt), *Czech Plays: Seven New Works* (edited by Marcy Arlin, Gwynn MacDonald and Daniel Gerould), *Playwrights before the Fall* (edited by Daniel Gerould), *Timbre4* (edited and translated by Jean Graham-Jones), *Jan Fabre: The Servant of Beauty and I Am a Mistake* (edited and foreword by Frank Hentschker), *Quick Change: 28 Theatre Essays and 4 Plays in Translation* (by Daniel Gerould), *Shakespeare Made French: Four Plays by Jean-François Ducis* (edited and translated by Marvin Carlson), and *New Plays from Spain: Eight Works by Seven Playwrights* (edited by Frank Hentschker).

IN MEMORIAM: Daniel Gerould (1928–2012), MESTC Director of Publications
Martin E. Segal (1916–2012), MESTC Founder

www.ingramcontent.com/pod-product-compliance
Lightning Source LLC
Chambersburg PA
CBHW051056230426
43667CB00013B/2320